ZESHIN

The Catherine and Thomas Edson Collection

Introduction
Joe Earle

Catalogue
Sebastian Izzard

San Antonio Museum *of* Art

Cover:
no. 23 (detail)

Frontispiece:
no. 5, interior of
lid (detail)

This publication is issued in conjunction with the exhibition
*The Genius of Shibata Zeshin: Selections from the Catherine
and Thomas Edson Collection*, held at the

San Antonio Museum of Art
February 17, 2007 – May 6, 2007

The Minneapolis Institute of Arts
October 13, 2007 – January 6, 2008

Designer: Miki Aoyagi

Photographers: Peggy Tenison (nos. 3–6, 8, 19, 22, 23, 26–31,
33–46, 48, 50, 52, 53); John Deane (nos. 1, 2, 7, 24, 25, 32, 47,
49, 51); Douglas Chew Ho (nos. 9–18, 20, 21)

Typesetter: Brandy Young

Printed and bound by Pressroom Printer & Designer,
Hong Kong

Library of Congress Control Number: 2006940901
ISBN: 978-1-883502-14-0 (paperback)
ISBN: 978-1-883502-15-7 (hardcover)

CONTENTS

DIRECTOR'S FOREWORD

With the inauguration of the Lenora and Walter F. Brown Asian Art Wing in May of 2005, the San Antonio Museum of Art declared its commitment to collect, preserve, and exhibit the very best of the arts of China, Japan, and other Asian countries. Paralleling that commitment, we are also dedicated to the periodic organization of exhibitions that complement our permanent displays. Kay and Tom Edson, already generous contributors to our Asian program, have now loaned us their important collection of paintings and art objects created by Shibata Zeshin (1807–1891), one of the foremost Japanese artists of the nineteenth century. Working in two mediums, painting and lacquer, Zeshin constantly strove to preserve ancient techniques while, at the same time, experimenting to push his art to new levels of excellence, sophistication, and beauty. The Edsons' carefully compiled collection of some fifty works by the master is notable for its superb quality and broad representation of Zeshin's remarkable oeuvre.

Our curator of Asian Art, Martha Blackwelder, expertly served as project director for the exhibition and, as ever, she did a superb job. Joe Earle, Matsutaro Shoriki Chair of the Department of Art of Asia, Oceania, and Africa at the Museum of Fine Arts, Boston, has provided an illuminating survey of Zeshin's career to serve as an introduction to the exhibition's contents. Sebastian Izzard, a specialist in Japanese art, curated the exhibition and wrote the catalogue. His involvement with SAMA over the decades has been enormously valuable to the success of our Asian program. Once again, we are fortunate to have had designer Clifford LaFontaine work with Martha and our exhibitions team in producing an installation sensitive to the special aesthetic and practical needs of the Zeshin material.

We are indeed honored to have this collection in our charge and proud to be able to present it for the first time to the San Antonio public and later to other cities in the United States through a national tour.

Marion Oettinger, Jr., Ph.D.
Director
San Antonio Museum of Art

COLLECTORS' FOREWORD

Growing up in San Antonio did not offer many opportunities to be exposed to Japanese art. It was there, no doubt, brought back by servicemen after the war in the Pacific and the Occupation of Japan, but it was not a common sight and we did not come across it.

In the 1960s Kay's mother, Catherine Halff, built a new house and with it came a pair of six-panel Japanese screens. The architect had acquired these from another client and found the perfect spot for them in what was to become her living room. He built the screens in, and they looked grand mounted along the wall. At the time we had no idea what was depicted. We were just intrigued by the small, exotic scenes peopled by doll-like figures. Now we know the scenes to be late seventeenth-century Sumiyoshi school illustrations of the *Tales of Ise*, a collection of short tales and anecdotes once attributed to Ariwara no Narihira (825–880), a middle-ranking bureaucrat of the Heian court. After Catherine Halff's death in 1995, we placed the screens on loan in the San Antonio Museum of Art, and finally gave them to the museum in her memory in 2005.

The screens stimulated our interest in Asian art and launched us on our career as collectors. Our first purchase was a cloisonné enamel vase bought from an itinerant auction that we visited by chance. There were no other bidders for the lot, and we waved our hands only when told by the auctioneer that it was a bargain. We still have the vase. From this modest start, we began to acquire other cloisonné works, both Japanese and Chinese. We found, though, that we appreciated the workmanship and subject matter of the Japanese pieces more, and Japan and its arts became our main focus.

By now we had realized the limitations of Texas as a source for our collection and decided to look farther afield. A major step was to order sale catalogues from Sotheby's, which in the seventies was holding regular auctions of Japanese art in New York, and later from Christie's. We began to study the types of works that were available and to track the market. In the early eighties, we were aided in our endeavors by the arrival of James Godfrey as consulting curator of Asian Art in the San Antonio Museum. He encouraged us to trust our own tastes and instincts, and our modest collection began to grow, expanding from a few cloisonné items to include decorative metal boxes and containers, Satsuma earthenware ceramics, and finally lacquer.

In Japan the production of lacquer reached a level of expertise unmatched by any other country. So famous was the product and so widely imitated that in the seventeenth century, the term "japanned" in English came to mean a lacquered surface in the Japanese style, or at least a simulated one. We discovered genuine lacquer by the chance purchase of a book on the subject, which revealed to us a new world where skill and artistry were paramount. We were completely hooked and began to purchase lacquer in abundance. James helped us in organizing exhibitions of our acquisitions. The first, held at the San Antonio Museum in 1984, then traveled to the Phoenix Art Museum in Arizona, and from there to a larger venue at the Minneapolis Institute of Arts.

In lacquer we did not concentrate on one area, content as we were to enjoy the miniature pleasures of *inrō*, the small, tiered containers once employed by the Japanese in lieu of pockets, while still acquiring larger writing and document boxes. Rapidly, this area of our collection overtook the others.

Our first encounter with Zeshin was not auspicious. Japanese art is generally signed, which presents the problem of authenticity. We purchased two *inrō* supposedly by the master, but on closer study, the signatures turned out to be false and the *inrō* had to be returned. The next purchase we made was a pair of paintings by Zeshin, depicting an eagle glaring at its reflection in a waterfall, and it was through paintings that our first real encounter with the artist occurred.

In 1994 we had the great good fortune to see Japan ourselves. We went as part of a tour organized by the Brooklyn Museum of Art, led by its able curator of Asian art, Amy Poster. It was a whirlwind trip through museums and famous sites, and included visits to a number of prominent art dealers both in Tokyo and in Kyoto. We were exposed to many beautiful works of art of types that we had not seen before and made a number of acquisitions that remain among our treasures. This encouraged our budding interest in painting, and the range of our collection broadened even further.

As we live in a dry climate, where the threat of drought is omnipresent, we were drawn to paintings of waterfalls, of which Zeshin made many. We purchased a number, not only by Zeshin but by other artists as well. Despite the earlier disappointment, we now began to acquire lacquer by the master, the first example being a tray decorated with lotus. Several other pieces soon arrived. One of the earliest was a set of food containers decorated with a river and waterwheel design. It is a work upon which Zeshin lavished all his skills and is the high point of our collection. Focusing on one artist took some time, but we realized that in Zeshin we had found someone to whom we responded. Not only were we impressed by his evident technical skills; we were also amused by his playfulness and sense of whimsy, and attracted by his love of nature. The variety of his work impressed us, and we decided to make a representative collection, for his skills were in both the areas of Japanese art we had grown to love, painting and lacquerware.

The collection grew quickly. Zeshin's lacquer paintings seemed to embody the features of his work that we most enjoyed, and we were fortunate in being able to acquire a number of unusual and beautiful examples in this medium, both in the format of hanging scrolls and as albums of small images. Now it seems that the collection has become one of the richest in this particular aspect of Zeshin's creativity.

Now that the collection is about to be exhibited, it gives us great pleasure to acknowledge the individuals who have helped both in forming it and in presenting it to a wider public for their enjoyment. Marion Oettinger, Director of the San Antonio Museum of Art, and Martha Blackwelder, Maddux-Cowden-Brown Curator of Asian Art at the museum, have throughout been generous and informed supporters of the project. To the exhibition designer Clifford LaFontaine, we owe our thanks for its beautiful installation. Our thanks are also due to James Godfrey, who, as we mentioned before, guided us in our early years as collectors and continues to be a fount of good advice. For their role in helping to build the collection we are grateful to Joan Mirviss, from whom we acquired the pair of eagle paintings by Zeshin referred to above, and Sebastian Izzard, whom we first met as an auction-house specialist, and who later used his resources to channel in our direction many of the choice pieces in the collection.

Drawing on his knowledge of the collection, Sebastian Izzard has now written the present informative catalogue. Our thanks are due to him and his production team, as they are to Joe Earle, Matsutaro Shoriki Chair of the Department of Art of Asia, Oceania, and Africa at the Museum of Fine Arts, Boston, an authority on Japanese lacquer and on Zeshin, for his perceptive introduction. In particular, we are grateful to the designer of the catalogue, Miki Aoyagi, who has been involved with the project since the beginning and has been tireless in her commitment to do justice to Zeshin's achievement.

Kay and Tom Edson
San Antonio, December 2006

INTRODUCTION

Joe Earle

More a lingering Edo blossom than a flower of Meiji…

Kawasaki Chitora 1897[1]

Shibata Zeshin (1807–1891) was one of the most unusual Japanese artists of the nineteenth century. Not only did he achieve almost equal fame as a painter of silk or paper scrolls and as a lacquerer of boxes and trays, something no one had done before, he even invented a type of "lacquer painting" (*urushi-e*)—well represented in the Edson Collection (nos. 44–53)—that enabled him to combine both of those ancient arts. He devised a host of other new lacquer techniques and deployed them on a wide array of objects to create a visual world so distinctive that there is normally no need to search for his tiny signature, often scratched with a rat's tooth in the dark surface. He is unusual, too, not just for his artistic singularity but also for the skewed chronological spread of his output. Although we know a good deal about the techniques he invented during the 1840s and we have a few records of commissions carried out in the same decade, apparently only a handful of his surviving works predate 1868, the last year of the Edo period (1615–1868) and the first of the Meiji era (1868–1912). His reputation rests, therefore, on lacquerware, paintings, and lacquer paintings executed during the last quarter century of his life, when Japan experienced some of the most profound and far-reaching changes in her long history.

In 1867–68 the military government of the shoguns was overthrown by a coalition of reformist samurai from the west of the country, and the teenage emperor Mutsuhito was installed as a constitutional monarch ruling from Zeshin's native city of Tokyo (formerly known as Edo), which replaced Kyoto as the national capital. These changes, and Zeshin's reaction to them, have helped to fashion two contradictory ideas of his place in the history of Japanese art. He often

No. 25 (detail)

worked as a reluctant, though not wholly unwilling, servant of a revolutionary government that, immediately after his death, responded by hailing him as a savior and reformer of traditional crafts. Throughout much of the twentieth century, however, he was virtually ignored by his countrymen, regarded as either a minor late representative of the Maruyama-Shijō style of painting or, worse still, just another Meiji-era artisan whose work, compromised by slavish pandering to Victorian taste, owed little to traditional Japanese ideas of design. In the West, especially in Great Britain, he was already admired for his lacquer during his lifetime, and in more recent decades his foreign fans, mostly Americans, have held him up as a stern perfectionist and wellspring of authentic Japanese culture, preserving strict workshop discipline and meticulous technique in a period of artistic decline: a source of reassuring stability, perhaps, in our own uncertain times. Neither stereotype—export-oriented government stooge nor diehard traditionalist—does this great artist justice. Certainly, Zeshin was a conservative in some things, but it is only when we consider carefully the paradoxical nature of his conservatism that a clearer picture of his real personality emerges. A glance at the chief events of his long career helps clarify some of the concerns that motivated the vast and distinctive artistic production of his last decades.

Zeshin was born into the heart of the Edo handicraft industry[2]—one of the largest and most sophisticated such industries of premodern times, and one that serviced the world's most populous city, with more than one million inhabitants. His father was originally from a family of carpenters (a part of his background that may be alluded to in the decoration of no. 14) but had been adopted by a maker of tobacco pouches. At the age of eleven Zeshin was apprenticed to the lacquerer Koma Kansai II (1766–1835), the head of a craft dynasty that had flourished for nearly two centuries, supplying both shoguns and emperors, as well as the burgeoning middle class of Edo and the other great cities, with decorated stationery boxes, picnic sets, bowls, cosmetic sets, *inrō* (miniature tiered medicine containers), and other luxury goods. In Kansai's atelier, Zeshin would have learned about the many stages that are involved in the creation of a piece of Japanese lacquerware: careful preparation of the wood or paper core; refining the raw sap of the lacquer tree; coloring and applying numerous coats of lacquer, allowing each of them to set in optimal conditions of heat and relative humidity; polishing each coat in several stages before applying the next one; manufacturing gold, silver, and other metal foils, flakes, and powders; shaking and/or laying these onto a still-damp lac-

quer surface to create a *maki-e* (literally, "sprinkled picture") design; applying a further coat or coats of lacquer; and polishing the finished product, again in several stages with a range of abrasives (fig. 1).

Kansai's workshop enjoyed a high reputation for mastery of these complex, time-consuming processes, but the early nineteenth century was not a time of great artistic innovation in lacquer. Zeshin's creative ambitions were such that at the early age of sixteen he decided to enter the studio of a painting master, Suzuki Nanrei (1775–1844), later moving to Kyoto and studying with Okamoto Toyohiko (1773–1845). As noted above, very few of Zeshin's earlier paintings survive, but the Edson collection includes several that were brushed late in his life, during the 1880s. These compositions remind us how deep were Zeshin's roots in mid-Edo period culture, not just in his choice of subjects such as waterfalls (nos. 36–38) or tigers (no. 39) that were pioneered or favored by the great painter Maruyama Ōkyo (1733–1795; fig. 2, and no. 46-2),[3] but also in his emulation of that master's blend of Western naturalism and East Asian brushwork. Toyohiko was a pupil of Matsumura Goshun (1752–1811), a leading artist who counted Ōkyo among his teachers, and who is credited with the foundation of the "Maruyama-Shijō" school, Shijō Street in Kyoto being the location of Goshun's atelier. Toyohiko's other principal teacher was the haiku poet and "literati" painter Yosa Buson (1716–1783), and elements of the painting style of both Buson and Ōkyo were passed on to Zeshin by Toyohiko. The soft textures and atmospheric colors of *Entrance to a Country Temple in Autumn* (no. 40) closely reflect Buson's manner and are seen in many works by Zeshin in other collections.

Impressive as these paintings are, it is unlikely that Zeshin would be as celebrated as he is today had he allowed his passion for brush and ink to prevent him from returning to Edo to follow his original calling as a lacquer artist. We have few details concerning his life between 1840 and the start of the Meiji era, but it is clear that, especially during the 1840s, he devoted much time to developing novel lacquer techniques that would enable him to take the medium to a new expressive level. While there was doubtless an artistic impulse behind this intense period of research and development, economic and political

Figure 1

Hasegawa Mitsunobu (act. 1730–60), View of lacquer workshop: turning bowls, applying lacquer, and putting trays of lacquered bowls in the drying ovens; from *Nippon sankai meibutsu zue* (Japanese famous products of land and sea), (1754); height 8½ in. (21.6 cm)

V&A Images/ Victoria and Albert Museum

considerations played a part as well. The 1830s and 1840s witnessed a prolonged economic crisis that spawned a series of clumsy government efforts to curb spending on luxuries, including laws restricting the incorporation of silver and gold in certain kinds of lacquer. In response, Zeshin developed techniques that used cheaper materials but required even more time and skill than conventional *maki-e* with precious metals.[4] The wave-patterned *seigaiha-nuri* ("blue sea waves lacquering") texture (nos. 2, 6, 25), supposedly not used since about 1700, involved drawing a comblike tool through a thin layer of wet lacquer previously mixed with cereal starch or white lead to improve its viscosity. The subdued dark-green ground *seidō-nuri* ("bronze lacquering"), seen to magnificent effect in the Edson document box (no. 3), was created by scattering bronze and charcoal (instead of gold and silver) dusts on the wet lacquer and polishing them with different oils and powders. Zeshin also found ways of simulating rusty iron (no. 24) and, most complex of all, *shitan* (Chinese rosewood; fig. 3, nos. 6, 7, 26). By the dawn of the Meiji era, with one important excep-

tion, he had perfected all of the new techniques that he would deploy so masterfully until his death. That exception was *urushi-e*, lacquer painting on paper or silk, using a brush instead of sprinkling on metal powders as in traditional *maki-e*.

An earlier lacquerer, Hara Yōyūsai (1772–1845/6), had painted a few fan leaves with black lacquer, but in 1873 Zeshin increased the technique's potential by devising ways of coloring lacquer without affecting its physical properties and adding substances that made it slightly flexible even when it had set, so that it could be applied to scrolls without flaking off when they were rolled and unrolled. The Edson collection includes many examples (nos. 47–53), but both in the collection and in Zeshin's overall oeuvre, *urushi-e* scrolls are easily outnumbered by works painted on the more reliable support provided by album leaves (nos. 44–46), suggesting that even the master was concerned about the long-term durability of the new medium. Happily, his fears were largely unfounded. While Zeshin's earlier innovations were inspired both by economic restrictions and the elusive aesthetic known as *iki*, to which we will return in a moment, according to an account by his son Reisai he developed *urushi-e* so as to achieve in lacquer the same effects as oils. If Reisai's recollection was correct, it is interesting that Zeshin did not use the new, viscous medium to create works that resembled Western painting in format, subject matter, or style, instead reserving it for some of his most delicate celebrations of traditional Japanese life and culture.

Figure 2

Maruyama Ōkyo (1733–95), *Waterfall*, hanging scroll, ink and light color on paper, 59⅛ x 34⅞ in. (150 x 88.5 cm)

The J. Sanford and Constance Miller Foundation (photo: Kaz Tsuruta)

Figure 3

Rosewood Drawer with a Metal Handle and Cleated Crack, album leaf, lacquer on paper (no. 45-14)

The leaders of the Meiji government took measures to ensure that the arts, no less than religion, commerce, and agriculture, would play a full part in ambitious plans to create a modern nation-state to rival the Western powers. They enlisted Zeshin almost immediately, in 1869 commissioning him to decorate thirty chairs with gold-lacquer cherry blossom for the imperial palace and in 1872 ordering a ceremonial riding crop for the emperor's personal use. Although neither of these commissions has survived, we can only surmise that Zeshin was selected not just because of his technical prowess (many other more conventional lacquerers were available) but because there was something about his style that suited the aims of Japan's new rulers. Perhaps these works were decorated in a similar manner

critical reception, between rigid tradition and inventive, expressive craftsmanship.

Zeshin's formal, official career continued to develop right up to the year of his death. As well as serving on several government committees, he carried out many further public commissions. In 1885–86, for example, he decorated four cedarwood doors for the new Imperial palace buildings and, also during the 1880s, he collaborated with his son Shinsai in producing one hundred and twelve floral roundel designs for the ceiling of the Chigusa no Ma, a formal hall within the palace complex.[6] Finally, at the end of 1890, just a few months before his death, he was named Teishitsu Gigeiin (Artist to the Imperial Household), a title inaugurated in that year and awarded to ten artists, among whom Zeshin was the sole lacquerer. However, Zeshin did not work exclusively or even predominantly to government order or for government-sponsored expositions, important as official patronage was for the maintenance of what must have been a large atelier. Most of the pieces in the Edson collection and in several other private collections were produced by Zeshin and his workshop collaborators for private clients between about 1865 and his death in 1891.

As noted earlier, Zeshin's work was passed over by Japanese art historians for most of the twentieth century and apart from an official eulogy issued after his death, even those writers who do mention him make no reference to his achievements in lacquer. One exception to this was Fujioka Sakutarō (1870–1910), whose *Kinsei kaigashi* (History of painting in recent times) was first published in 1903 and often reprinted. Fujioka states that Zeshin's chief strength was in *maki-e* and recounts both the revival of *seigaiha-nuri* and the invention of *urushi-e*. He is also interesting in that he moves beyond the bland generalization that Zeshin worked in the Shijō style, observing that "by painting a few things so that they seem to overflow beyond the edges of the paper, he achieved the same emotional impact as the haiku master does with his little seventeen-syllable verses."[7] Fujioka applies this insight, the fruit perhaps of his background as a literary historian, to Zeshin's painting, but it could usefully describe his lacquers and *urushi-e* as well.

Zeshin himself was an accomplished haiku

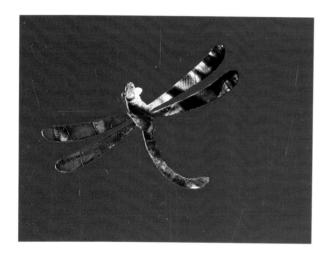

Figure 4

Lacquer tray with mother-of-pearl (*warigai*) decoration of insects, (no. 34, detail)

to the Kasuga picnic set in the Edson collection (no. 34), outwardly conservative in style and technique, but with the unexpected detail of two butterflies and a dragonfly in cut-shell inlay (*warigai*), a technique Zeshin is supposed to have developed after examining an old piece in 1881 (fig. 4).[5] Significantly, Zeshin signed the Kasuga set in red lacquer, using the surname of his lacquer teacher Koma Kansai, possibly in order to suggest that this was one of his more traditionalist works. The hard-edged black and gold of the tiered box evokes the formal world of the samurai more than any other piece in the Edson collection, but the inlaid insects add an unobtrusively subversive note that neatly encapsulates the dichotomy, both in Zeshin's work and in its poet, as the following examples show:

Kasa ni tsuku	Sitting on my hat
cho to hitotsu ni	Zeshin and a butterfly—
miyako iri	entering Kyoto.

Aki shimite	Autumn's chilly close
nokoru ya shimo no	lingering on a frosty branch—
karasu-uri	a snake-gourd.

And if miniaturization, understatement, and suggestion, hallmarks of haiku, can be used to characterize Zeshin's greatest and most distinctive work, so too can *iki*. This elusive concept has been defined as the quality of being "light and unconstrained, gallant but not obstinate, playful but never tiresome,"[8] while the theoretician Kuki Shūzō (1888–1941) stated that, in painting, *iki* would "place emphasis on the outlines, avoid rich colors, and be uncomplicated in structure." When it comes to color, Kuki also tells us that bright hues are not *iki*: colors that he regards as falling within the definition as *iki* include mouse or slate gray, yellowish brown, blackish brown among the browns, and dark blue and grayish blue among the blues; *urushi-nezumi* (lacquer gray) and *matsuba* (dark green) are also mentioned[9]—in other words, many of the subdued colors produced using Zeshin's new techniques that are seen on lacquerwares and lacquer paintings in the Edson collection (fig. 5). Again, Kuki considers the ultimate origins of *iki* to lie in skittish coquetry between the sexes, and there is much visual coquetry in Zeshin, much teasing of the eye when ingenious composition leads it from one side of a box to the next (no. 25) or from the outside to the inside (no. 5), or cleverly fools it into mistaking lacquer for wood, iron, or pewter (nos. 7, 24, 29). Although his love of rustication and ancient, worn surfaces, seen in the sword mounts and sword (nos. 22, 23), may well have been inspired by the aesthetics of the tea ceremony (another of Zeshin's cultural pursuits, see nos. 18 and 47) with its cult of *wabi* (loneliness, austerity) and *sabi* (patina, age), even this aspect of his art can be seen as a reflection of *iki*, especially perhaps when a rough, weathered surface is contrasted with accents of finely polished lacquer.

There is no doubting the importance of *iki* to Zeshin and in fact, quite apart from the visual

evidence of his work, what little we know about his private life shows him to have been on friendly terms with individuals who were regarded by their contemporaries as embodiments of either *iki* or the related concept of *tsū*, a term coming closer than *iki* to the English "cool."[10] *Iki* is such a slippery term, however, that there is a temptation to use it as a catchall describing everything that is most characteristic of Zeshin's work. One facet of his genius that may or not be covered by *iki*, but certainly deserves special mention, is his melancholy celebration of tradition, be it that of his own and other crafts or of the very fabric of Edo-period life, which Zeshin knew to be fading away just as his own life drew to a close. He was an activist antiquarian and conservationist, busily sketching the ancient sculptures of Nara (Japan's capital in the seventh and eighth centuries), using his own money to prevent the dispersal of a set of medieval portrait paintings, and later participating in government-commissioned surveys of ancient art. But his greatest loyalty was perhaps not so much to the great traditions of Buddhist iconography, temple architecture, or landscape painting as to the humbler traditions of his native Edo and its artisanal industries. Time and again he lovingly re-creates a craft process, be it the manufacture of clay dolls' heads (no. 48), the decoration of shells (no. 49), ceramic glazes (nos. 18, 47), the chiseling of metal sword ornaments (nos. 12, 13), or a

Figure 5

Green, yellow-brown, and dark brown colors used by Zeshin considered *iki*, (no. 1, detail)

previous lacquerer's imitations of Chinese ink cakes (fig. 8 and nos. 9–11). Zeshin certainly did not neglect such time-honored themes as the seasonal plants depicted in the brilliantly eclectic tiered box (no. 25), but he seems to have been even more drawn to popular festivals and religious beliefs, both urban and rural (as in nos. 3, 12, 35, 48, 49 among others).

Zeshin's understated, unassuming cataloguing of Edo culture (a feature especially of his albums of small-scale lacquer paintings), never sentimental, always with an edge of humorous, *iki*, elegance, perhaps holds the key to his dual reputation as both conservative and reformer. The pompous wording of his posthumous official eulogy presents him merely as a technical innovator and organizer, falsely stating that the art of lacquering "had in recent times become crude and weak and . . . *maki-e* craftsmanship fell far short of ancient times."[11] This was a canard widely put about by the Meiji government, and applied also to mediums other than lacquer, no doubt in order to stress its own role in the revival of Japan's craft industries while downplaying the fact that so many of them had changed radically in response to the demands of art bureaucrats and foreign buyers. Yet if Zeshin had been predominantly an export-oriented technical wizard in the same way as Suzuki Chōkichi (1848–

1919) in bronze casting, Miyagawa Kōzan (1842–1916) in porcelain, or Kawashima Jinbei (1853–1910) in tapestry weaving—all of them craft-entrepreneurs of the following generation—it is doubtful that he would have been so much loved in the West, both in his own time and ours. Zeshin was disingenuous in portraying his frugal use of precious metals as a matter of patriotism, once stating that "gold and silver are the nation's most precious treasures; to apply them recklessly results in bad decoration and shows lack of regard for the national interest."[12] In reality, the understatement that stemmed from his frugality with materials was the perfect expression of *iki*, a state of mind that in the late Edo period was a subversive counter to the swagger of samurai culture, but struck a backward-looking note in the heady, modernizing climate of the early Meiji years. Therein lies the essence of Zeshin's conservatism and his wistful, vignetted glimpses of an irrecoverable past.

1. Kawasaki (1897), p. 3; author's translation.
2. The biographical details given here are drawn from Umezawa (1996).
3. For Zeshin's reputation as an expert authenticator of Ōkyo's work, see Dilworth and Rimer, eds. (1977), p. 365.
4. For Zeshin's technical innovations, see Earle (1996).
5. Umezawa (1996), p. 52.

6. Yokomizo and Satsuma (2005), passim.

7. Fujioka (1910), p. 334; Fujioka suggests earlier (p. 239) that the haikulike flavor of Zeshin's art might owe something to the influence of Rinpa painter Sakai Hōitsu (1761–1828).

8. Gōke (1981b), p. 5.

9. Kuki (1930), pp. 107–8.

10. See Dilworth and Rimer, eds. (1977), p. 363.

11. Umezawa (1996), p. 50.

12. Ibid., p. 52.

Figure 8

Shibata Zeshin (1807–1891), *Horsefly on Ink-cake, Paper-Wrapped Ink Stick*, (no. 46–1). Signed *Tairyūkyo Zeshin sha* and sealed *Koma*

LACQUERWARE

Lacquer, *urushi* in Japanese, is derived from the sap of the lacquer tree (*Rhus verniciflua*), a deciduous tree of the sumac family indigenous to China and Japan. Its application is an art that requires skill, patience, and care. Like North American poison ivy, its sap has a toxic element that adds to the difficulties of handling it, making this a hazardous and time-consuming process. For best results lacquer must be applied in a thin layer, and then allowed to harden in a drying cabinet before it is ready for the next coat. The higher the quality desired the more layers are applied, and for objects of the highest quality, thirty or so layers may be used. The shaping, joinery, and preparation of an object are also painstaking, even exclusive of its decoration, and months or even years of intermittent labor may be required to ensure that warping and cracking do not occur. Lacquer is therefore an expensive product, for in order to manufacture wares in a timely fashion a carefully organized schedule is needed, with work completed in tandem with other projects. In turn, this requires the use of teams of specialists to carry out the various stages of its production.

Once hardening has taken place, a lustrous and extremely durable coating is achieved, which serves as an effective sealant. Lacquer was originally developed for utensils used in the serving, storage, and preservation of food, for it is resistant to heat and even to mild chemical abrasives, and is impervious to liquid. It can also be made into airtight containers, effective as insect-proof storage for clothes, valuables, and documents. The useful properties of lacquer seem to have been recognized in China and Japan as early as the second millennium B.C.

As the use of lacquer increased, so did the desire to embellish it. Coloring agents, such as vermilion for red and lampblack or iron filings for black, were introduced, as were shell and twisted wire inlay for decoration, a step thought to have been imported from Korea. Lacquer is an excellent adhesive, and can also be effectively decorated with applied metal powders, metal leaf, sheet metal, mother-of-pearl, ceramic, glass, and other materials.

During the Edo period (1615–1868), the long peace encouraged a growth in urban consumer spending. Conspicuous expenditure on luxury items led to the development of more and more elaborate decoration for such personal accessories as sword scabbards and *inrō*, the latter having made their first appearance during the preceding Momoyama period (1573–1615). *Inrō* are interlocking stacks of miniature containers to carry items such as medicines, powders, amulets, and seals, which the owner suspended from his obi by means of a netsuke, or toggle. Evolving styles and tastes meant that, by the early nineteenth century, the range and complexity of decorative techniques available to a lacquer master had reached its peak.

When Zeshin joined the Koma school headed by Kansai II in 1817, it was competing with a number of other lacquer families. Dating back to the seventeenth century, the Koma school was particularly well placed, having special arrangements with the shogunal authorities for the production of sets of boxes and utensils necessary for important ceremonies and events such as weddings.

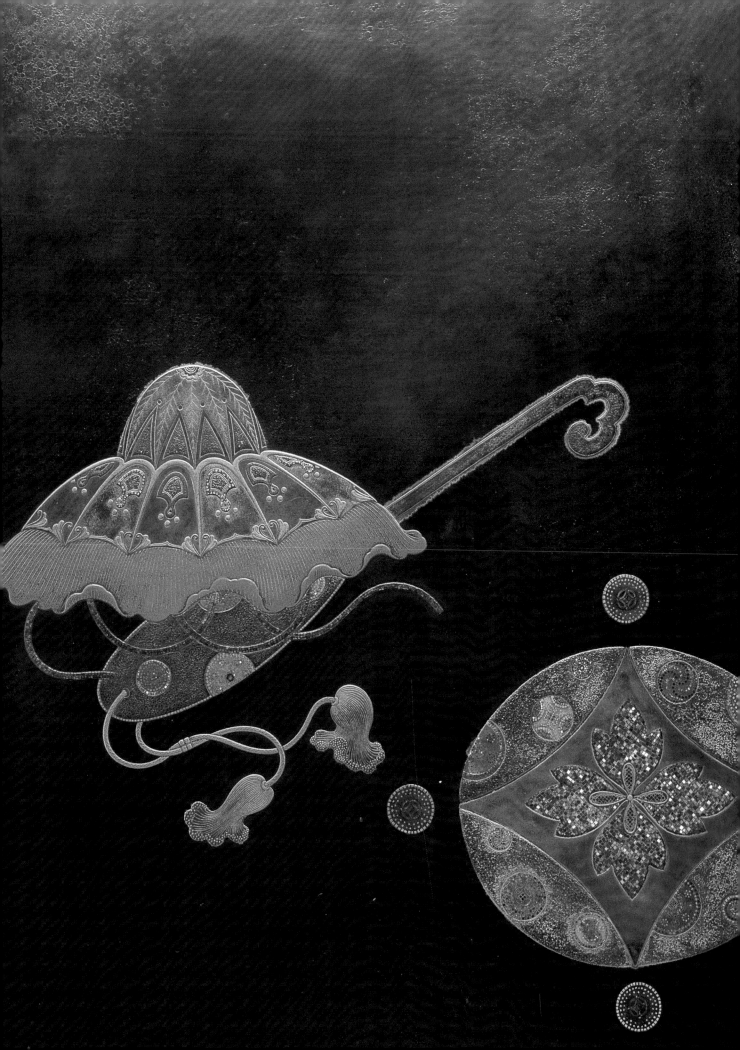

1 Document Box (*fubako*) with bamboo leaves

Green lacquer over wood; decorated in black and gold lacquer with mother-of-pearl highlights, the same decoration extending to the natural bamboo lid; 9⅜ x 2⅛ x 1¼ in. (23.8 x 5.4 x 3.2 cm); ca. 1860–90
Signature: *Zeshin* in scratched characters

One of the earliest uses of lacquer was for the protection and preservation of documents. This narrow, elegant box was made to contain either a small handscroll or a folded document, or perhaps even to hold brushes. The green tea-dust surface of the body is embellished in black and gold lacquer in a variety of textures. The design, of fresh and old, broken, and insect-eaten bamboo leaves, extends over the entire box, including the bamboo lid. This understated type of design and the unassuming material of the lid became fashionable among sophisticates following the sumptuary edicts enacted by the shogunal authorities during the 1840s, and the combination of lacquer and bamboo was much favored by Zeshin, who used it for a number of boxes in addition to *tonkotsu* (tobacco containers) and netsuke.

Gōke illustrates the plan of a similar document box with bamboo-leaf decoration, which was once in the collection of metal artist Kagawa Katsuhiro (1853–1917), who studied painting under Zeshin. The box itself is illustrated in the catalogue of the 1908 Zeshin memorial exhibition.[1]

1. Gōke (1981a), vol. 2, no. 287; Shioda, ed. (1908), n.p. (11th leaf from the back, lower left).

Previous page:
no. 3 (detail)

2 Stationery Box (*ryōshibako*) with treasures of the shoreline

Colored lacquer over wood; decorated with
incising and low relief; 6¼ x 9½ x 3⅛ in. (17.1 x
24.1 x 7.9 cm); ca. 1860–90
Signature: *Zeshin* in scratched characters
Published: Honolulu Academy of Arts (1996),
no. 67, pp. 154–55

This rectangular box with sloping sides and
overhanging lid is very much in the quiet and
refined taste that is one element of Zeshin's style.
It was once probably part of a set, together with
a writing box and possibly a table. The restrained
decoration of this deep brown container for
documents, which extends over the lid and two
sides, simulates waves on a shell-strewn shore.
The waves are combed in the *seigaiha-nuri* technique; seashells are scratched into the surface;
and the green seaweed blends in with the background.

The treasures of the seashore are a constant
theme in Zeshin's work. The artist seems to have
found particular satisfaction in depicting the
shells, colored pebbles, and strands of seaweed
that wash up along the beach, using these images
not only for lacquer objects but also for lacquer
paintings and screens.[1]

1. See, e.g., Shioda, ed. (1908), n.p. (26th leaf from the back),
detail of a six-panel screen; (20th leaf from the back), a two-
panel table screen.

3 Stationery Box (*ryōshibako*) with attributes of the Seven Gods of Good Fortune

Colored lacquer over wood; decorated in black and gold lacquer with mother-of-pearl highlights; 14 x 10½ x 4½ in. (35.6 x 26.7 x 11.4 cm); ca. 1860–70
Signature: *Zeshin*, with *kakihan*, both in scratched characters

This large, rectangular stationery box with sloping sides and overhanging lid is a form that Zeshin seems to have been particularly fond of (for another example, see no. 2). The flamboyant decoration is in contrast to that of the preceding box, and represents yet another facet of Zeshin's art. It may have been made for exhibition purposes only, rather than for actual use. The dark green lacquer surface is textured to imitate the surface of bronze (*seidō-nuri*) and is decorated with a variety of colors, metallic pigments, and inlays with a design symbolizing the *takaramono*, the myriad treasures associated with the Seven Gods of Good Fortune. According to Chinese and Japanese belief, these treasures were useful in achieving a long and healthy life.

On the lid are the vest of invisibility, a weight, and an elaborately rendered brocade ball. On the sides are the cloak of invisibility, another brocade ball, wish-granting gems, a scroll, and the mallet used by Daikoku, the God of Wealth. The interior of the lid is decorated with a Chinese fan, more gems, and auspicious abstract symbols.

Zeshin made a number of sets of document and writing boxes featuring this theme. The Khalili Collection has a set with a red ground and a box with a ground similar to that of the present example. These have been dated to 1860–70.[1]

1. Earle, ed. (1996), nos. 1–3.

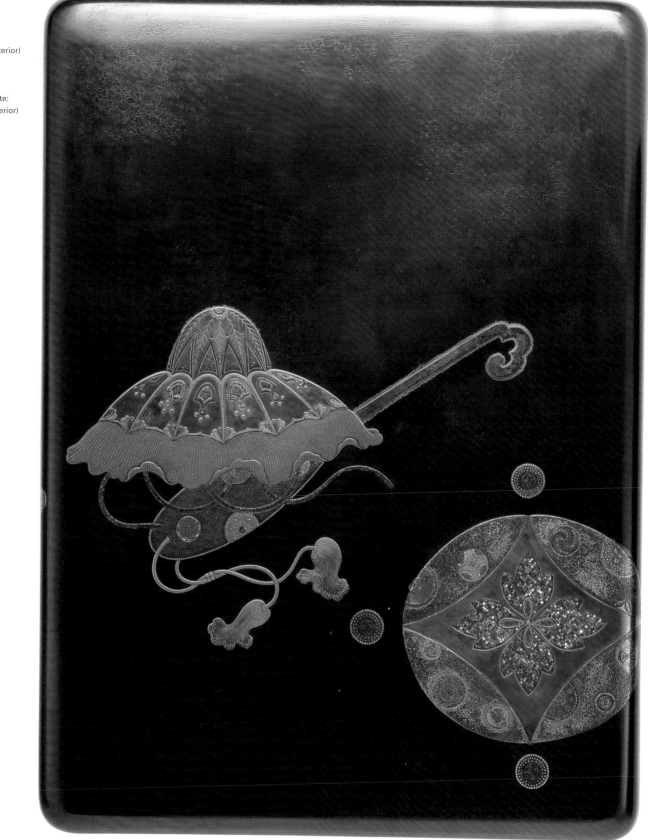

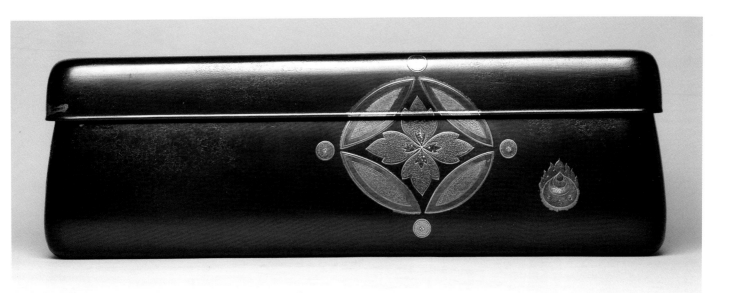

4 Document Box (*fubako*) with fruiting loquats

Colored lacquer over leather; decorated in colored and gold lacquer on a simulated dark bronze ground, with attached leather strap with metal fitting; 8⅝ x 2¼ x 1 in. (21.9 x 5.7 x 2.5 cm); ca. 1860–90
Signature: *Zeshin* in scratched characters

Zeshin had a wide range of visual imagery available to him. Here, in his depiction of the leaf and branch of the loquat tree, a member of the rose family originating in China, he has blended the objective realism which formed the basis of the Maruyama painting style he had studied in Kyoto with a stylized, flattened, Rinpaesque composition. Like the rotted bamboo leaves of no. 1, the over-ripe fruit falling to the ground, employed to balance the composition, is a touch typical of Zeshin's wry sense of humor and serves to enliven the design. The color of the loquat, a dark burnt-orange, is very much the type of *iki* hue that Zeshin favored.[1]

This leather-strapped lacquer box was probably made as a dispatch case for important papers. Although the shape is rare, a number of examples are known. One, decorated with a variety of different leaves, is now in the collection of the Tokyo National University of Fine Arts and Music; two others in the same format are illustrated in the 1908 catalogue of the exhibition held the previous December by the Committee for the Exhibition of Works by the Venerable Zeshin (*Zeshin-o isaku tenrankai*) to memorialize Zeshin on the seventeenth anniversary (by Japanese calculation) of his death.[2]

1. For a discussion of *iki*, see the Introduction.
2. See Gōke (1981a), vol. 1, pl. 28; and Shioda, ed. (1908), n.p. (12th leaf from the back, lower register): one, decorated with a gong and striker, once owned by Kawanobe Itchō (1830–1910), a well-known lacquerer of the Kōami School; and another featuring a design of autumnal plants. See also Gōke (1981a), vol. 2, nos. 286, 290, for layout plans of two similar containers described as document boxes (*fubako*), one with a design of persimmon leaves, the other with a gong and striker, taken from a publication dated Taishō 5 (1916).

5 Writing Box (*suzuribako*) with design of eggplants

Lacquer over wood and gauze base, rectangular form and beveled edges; decorated in black *hiramaki-e* with silver highlights, interior with insects among grasses in *hiramaki-e*, fitted with a copper alloy water-dropper in the form of a gourd; 7⅞ x 5⅜ x 1⅜ in. (20 x 13.7 x 3.5 cm); ca. 1860–70
Signature: *Zeshin* in raised black lacquer

Pre-Meiji lacquer works by Zeshin are rare. This writing box is accompanied by a storage box signed in Zeshin's characteristic calligraphy. The shape and the lacquer decoration have more in common with works known to date from the Edo period, such as a box decorated with Benkei stealing the bell of Mii Temple, which is dated Bunkyō 2 (1862),[1] and do not conform with the smooth, rounded corners and sophisticated finish normally associated with Zeshin's Meiji-era work.

1. Gōke (1981a), vol. 1, pl. 31.

No. 5
Interior

6 Writing Box (*suzuribako*) with Mount Tsukuba

Lacquer over a wood base, rectangular form; decorated with a simulated rosewood (*shitan-nuri*) surface and black *kanshitsu* and *seigaiha-nuri* details, the top and inside of the lid inscribed with a poem in gold lacquer, a simulated crack and repair of the lid at upper right; 10 x 9¼ x 1½ in. (25.4 x 23.5 x 3.8 cm); ca. 1860–90
Signature: *Zeshin sha* in gold lacquer

Zeshin's image is Mount Tsukuba, a mountain with twin peaks known as Nyotai-zan and Nantai-zan, in Hitachi Province, approximately forty miles northeast of Edo, shown here with low bands of mist above the river flowing at its base. Zeshin would have passed by the mountain in 1841 when, with Ikeda Taishin (1825?–1903) and other students, he retraced the famous pilgrimage undertaken by the master *haikai* poet Matsuo Bashō (1644–1694) in 1689, along the route that Bashō later called the *Narrow Road to the Deep North* (*Oku no hosomichi*).

Written in cursive calligraphy, an inscription in gold lacquer split between the outer and inner surfaces of the lid of this writing box is signed: *Ransetsu ku, Tōsei sho / Zeshin sha* (verse by Ransetsu, calligraphy by Tōsei, copied by Zeshin). Hattori Ransetsu (1654–1707), a samurai from Edo, was one of Bashō's top pupils. Tōsei (written with characters meaning "unripe peach") was a sobriquet sometimes used by Bashō ("plantain tree") after the 1670s. The inscription, therefore, informs the viewer that Zeshin has transcribed a poem by Ransetsu originally included in a manuscript brushed by Bashō.

The source of the poem was an account of a journey to Kashima (*Kashima kikō*), a journey the poetry master made, with Ransetsu and a few close pupils, two years before he traveled to the Deep North. The objective was to enjoy moon viewing at Kashima Shrine, about ten miles farther away from Edo than Mount Tsukuba. (Unfortunately, it was raining on the much-awaited night of the harvest moon).

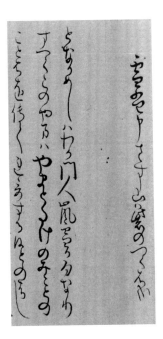

No. 6
Opposite page:
Lid, exterior and
interior

Left: Manuscript
of *Kashima kikō,*
taken from *Tenri
Toshokan zenpon
sōsho*

Right: Box interior

The poem reads:

yuki wa	Peaks capped with snow,
mōsazu	needless to say, are dazzling —
yama wa murasaki no	but behold Tsukuba tinged
Tsukuba kana	purple!

Ransetsu is suggesting that stunning as the snow-capped twin peaks of Mount Tsukuba might be in the winter, even more impressive is viewing them on an early spring morning, when they are veiled with bands of purple-tinged mist. We may be allowed to speculate that Zeshin decided to evoke the image of purple mountains on the surface of a Chinese rosewood (*shitan*) box because the word *shitan* is written with characters that mean literally "purple rosewood."

Rosewood was a luxury tropical hardwood imported into Japan from Southeast Asia by the Dutch during the Edo period. Zeshin's box, however, is a simulation made of brown lacquer in various hues applied over a wood core. *Shitan-nuri* (rosewood lacquer) was one of the most complex surfaces that Zeshin invented. He is thought to have developed it during the 1840s

and 1850s.[1] The realistic treatment is enhanced by scratching the fictive grain of the wood into the lacquer surface, a technique in which a rat's tooth is thought to have been used.

The verse itself can be considered an independent *hokku*, even though it is written with extra syllables. Before *haikai* conventions became standardized, it was not unusual for poets of the early Danrin (Bashō) school to write poems with extra syllables or lines. Taking advantage here of the unorthodox prosodic structure, the artist separated the text, inscribing the first line on the top of the box lid and the remainder of the poem on its reverse. In doing so, he cleverly created a verbal-visual game in which the viewer first sees only the words *yuki wa*, which can be read as a riddle: "What about snow?" To discover the answer, one must lift the lid and turn it over to read the rest of the inscription.

Zeshin has also faithfully imitated Bashō's calligraphy, as demonstrated by comparing the rendition in gold lacquer on the writing box with that of the original brushed manuscript of *Kashima kikō* (no. 6a, far right column; from *Tenri Toshokan zenpon sōsho*), which is preserved

in the Tenri Central Library. Zeshin even copied Bashō's calligraphic style in the rendering of the phrase *Ransetsu ku* (verse by Ransetsu), found in the teacher's original manuscript (no. 6a, 2nd column from the right). We may assume, however, that Zeshin knew the work in a woodblock-printed facsimile, perhaps the 1790 edition or a later printing.[2]

1. For Zeshin's studies using this technique, see no. 45-14; and Earle, ed. (1996), no. 76, fig. 13. For its use in detailing, see no. 26.
2. Commentary, with transcription and translation of the verse, by John T. Carpenter.

7 Incense Box (*kōgō*) simulating a repaired Chinese-rosewood container

Lacquer over papier-mâché; 2 ⅞ x 3 ¾ x 1 in.
(7.3 x 9.5 x 2.5 cm); ca. 1860–90
Signature: *Zeshin* in scratched characters
Published: Lazarnick (1982), no. 1271; Honolulu Academy of Arts (1996), no. 74, pp. 168–69

Incense was first imported into Japan from India by Buddhist monks, via the Silk Road and China. In the inventory of the Shōsoin, the imperial treasure house in Nara, an entry for A.D. 768 lists a number of small silk pouches for incense storage and nine bags of incense for scenting clothes. Also included was a log of incense wood from which a piece was cut and given to Shogun Ashikaga Yoshimasa (1436–1490), under whose rule arts such as tea drinking (*sadō*), flower arranging (*kadō*), the Nō theater, and incense appreciation (*kōdō*) flourished. The appreciation of incense soon developed into an aesthetic cult, which by the nineteenth century had migrated from the ruling elites to the wealthy mercantile

class, the mainstay of Zeshin's market. As with the drinking of tea, the value placed on the various containers and utensils employed in the rituals of incense appreciation meant that a great deal of care and attention was lavished on their manufacture.

This is another example of the *shitan-nuri* technique that Zeshin developed in the 1840s. As in no. 6, Zeshin has simulated a crack in the lid that has undergone a skillful repair in the form of a butterfly-shaped cleat and a metal staple. The effect is to suggest that the box is a treasured family heirloom, lovingly repaired through the ages, and perfectly appropriate for the use to which it was put.

8 Incense Box (*kōgō*) with tiger

Lacquer over papier-mâché; rectangular form decorated in gold, silver, and black lacquer on a green tea-dust ground, the interior in black and silver lacquer; 3½ x 1¼ x ¾ in. (8.9 x 4.5 x 1.9 cm); ca. 1860–90
Signature: *Zeshin* in scratched characters

Zeshin executed many paintings of tigers (see no. 39), often using a style loosely derived from that of the Kyoto artist Maruyama Ōkyo, of whose work Zeshin was considered to have an expert knowledge. In this image of a seated tiger, facing the viewer and greatly foreshortened, Zeshin applied the gold and black lacquer with painterly brushstrokes. Zeshin would never have seen an actual tiger and would have had to rely on earlier paintings of the subject, or on a domestic cat as his model (see no. 46-3), although tiger skins were popular imports.

9 *Inrō* with Chinese ink-cakes and a seal

Lacquer over wood, four cases, of rectangular form and oval section; polished black surface, black high relief, and carved red lacquer detail, red lacquer interior; 3½ x 2⅜ x 1⅛ in. (8.9 x 6 x 2.9 cm); ca. 1860–90
Signature: *Zeshin* in scratched characters
Ojime: coral bead
Netsuke: ivory of an eagle

One of Zeshin's achievements as a lacquer artist was the revival of older techniques. The present *inrō* features relief representations of old, worn, and cracked Chinese ink-cakes: on the front,[1] rectangular, decorated in high relief with an eagle on a branch; on the back, circular, bearing the Chinese inscription *Li weng Dazhuang xie jing zhi mo* (Special writing ink for writing the Dazhuang Sutra), with the name *Fang Da'ao* and seal *Ji Lin*. Fang Da'ao was the original name of Fang Yulu, the author of the *Fang shi mopu* (The ink-cake manual of Mr. Fang), the inspiration for such designs. In making this allusion to Fang, Zeshin was also paying tribute to Ogawa Haritsu (1663–1747), who originated this type of *inrō*; his art name Ritsuō appears on a tablet to the right of the inscription,[2] while the red seal reads *Kan*, another of Haritsu's art names.

1. On this *inrō* and others by Zeshin in the Edson collection, his signature appears on the left of the base, ending beside the left cord hole (*himotoshi*). Accordingly, in terms of front and back, the *inrō* are discussed here with this configuration in mind.
2. For another *inrō* by Zeshin bearing a portion of the same inscription and the same signature tablet, see Eskenazi (1996), no. 34, p. 32.

10 *Inrō* in the form of a Chinese ink-cake

Lacquer over wood, two cases, of rectangular form and section; polished black lacquer surface and black lacquer in relief; 2⅝ x 2 x ⅝ in. (6.7 x 5.1 x 1.59 cm); ca. 1860–90
Signature: *Zeshin sha* in scratched characters
Ojime (not illustrated): cylindrical ivory, incised and stained with a bamboo design, signed *Mitsuhiro* (Ōhara Mitsuhiro, 1810–1875)

11 Tobacco container (*tonkotsu*) in the form of a Chinese ink-cake

Lacquer over wood, of rectangular form and section, containing a single tray with a handle carved as a horsefly; polished black lacquer, black relief decoration, polished black lacquer interior; 3 x 2 x ⅝ in. (7.6 x 5.1 x 1.59 cm); ca. 1860–90
Signature: *Zeshin* in scratched characters
Ojime: black lacquer bead
Netsuke: lacquer, en suite with the *tonkotsu*, in black relief simulating a used ink-stick with the design of a bat flying over auspicious fungus; signed: *Zeshin* in scratched characters

Unlike the preceding *inrō*, the design of a tethered horse from the imperial stables is directly derived from the *Fang shi mopu* (vol. 2, pl. 18r), where the ink-cake appears as octagonal (as it does in Zeshin's painted version; see no. 46-1). Zeshin adapted it to suit his own purposes. An inscription, *Ying tu qiu jun ma* (My wish is for a horse such as the one shown here) appears on the reverse in a rectangular cartouche. Several different versions of this *inrō* survive, and occasionally the inscription is surrounded by a decorative band containing musical instruments.[1]
A number of Zeshin's Ritsuō-style *sagemono* are found in European and American collections, and it seems likely that it was to such as these that the British designer Christopher Dresser (1834–1904) was referring when he commented in 1882, apropos of Ritsuō:

> Some works of this great manufacturer have come into this country. But the majority of the pieces which reach England are made by Ikede [*sic*] Zeshin, a man who still lives, and who has not only adopted the style of his predecessor, but makes deceptive imitations of the older work; even the cracks and chips of the old specimens being counterfeited.[2]

1. See Helmert-Corvey, ed. (1997), no. 94, pp. 148–49.
2. Dresser (1882), p. 352. Dresser appears to have confused Zeshin's name with that of his student and life-long collaborator Ikeda Taishin, assuming them perhaps to be the same person.
3. Dresser (1882), p. 352.

Like no. 10, this *tonkotsu* is derived from the *Fang shi mopu* (The ink-cake manual of Mr. Fang).[1] It is decorated in relief with a cropped detail of light emanating from a ceremonial vessel known as a *tan ting*, which was thought to be used by Taoist Immortals as a source of cinnabar. In thus alluding to Fang, Zeshin also records his debt to Ritsuō, the originator of this type of design, by including his *Kan* seal, which appears in relief at the lower left. On the back are Chinese seal characters reading *Hōrodai* (Ch: *Baolutai*), or Precious Dew Tower, a clichéd expression for an artist's studio. The name is probably based on the tower built by Han emperor Wu (r. 141–87 B.C.) to catch the early morning dew, the "moisture of the immortals." The horsefly that forms the handle is typical of Zeshin's slightly irreverent touch.

1. See Helmert-Corvey, ed. (1997), no. 95, p. 150. Several versions of this container exist as either *inrō* or *tonkotsu*: see Gōke (1981a), fig. 20; Meech (1995), no. 42, p. 88.

12 *Inrō* with *kozuka, fuchi,* and sword guard

Lacquer over wood, three cases, squared oval form and section; decorated in the round to simulate the texture and patina of a variety of metal surfaces, on a rich greenish gray ground imitating *shibuichi*; one side with a *kozuka* inscribed *Miboku*, engraved with cherry blossom in driving rain, and a dark copper *fuchi* inlaid with two ants in *shakudo* and a feather in *shibuichi* and gilt; the reverse with an iron *tsuba* inscribed *Yasuchika*, featuring plovers in flight over waves; the interior in bright gold lacquer; 3⅛ x 2⅜ x ⅞ in. (7.9 x 6 x 2.22 cm); ca. 1860–90
Signature: *Zeshin* in scratched characters
Ojime: *shakudo* and copper bead
Netsuke: lacquer box-type, the lid decorated with a rabbit pounding rice-cakes at New Year, in gold and silver *hiramaki-e* with inlaid shell details on a polished black ground; the case in *shitan-nuri* signed: *Zeshin* in scratched characters
Published: Stern (1972), no. 156, pp. 82–83; Gōke (1981a), vol. 1, no. 84

Both Tsuchiya Yasuchika (1670–1744) and Hamano Shōzui (1696–1769), known as Miboku, were leading Nara school makers of *machibori*-style sword-fittings in the early eighteenth century. This *inrō* is an example of Zeshin's ability to reproduce metal surfaces in lacquer, and he demonstrates his skill by simulating a variety of soft-metal alloys as well as iron.

13 *Inrō* with foxes' wedding party

Lacquer over wood, four cases, of rectangular form and oval section; silver lacquer carved in *katakiri-bori*, with black, red, and yellow lacquer details; gold *nashiji* interior; 3⅛ x 2 x ⅝ in. (7.9 x 5.1 x 1.59 cm); ca. 1860–90
Signature: *Zeshin* in scratched characters
Ojime: black lacquer bead form carved in low relief with scrolling flowers, gold and silver details
Netsuke: ivory carved as a fox shrine guardian

Zeshin's love of imitating unusual surfaces in lacquer is well known. Here, as in the preceding entry, he replicates a surface of *shibuichi*, an alloy of copper and silver, carved in *katakiri-bori*, a style of metal chasing which was the specialty of Yokoya Sōmin (1670–1733) and his eighteenth- and nineteenth-century followers. Colored lacquer has been applied in layers, finishing with a layer of silver lacquer; the design has then been carved through these surfaces at varying depths, revealing details in different hues.

Decorated in the round and beginning with the head of the column on the front, the design is typical of Zeshin's whimsical approach to Japanese folklore, in which foxes, believed to inhabit a parallel universe, hold a special place. People, especially children, were admonished to leave them alone and thought foolish to intervene in their affairs. Foxes guard Shinto shrines and serve as the messengers of the God of Rice. Legend has it that foxes' wedding processions—which, according to Japanese custom, are made up of a parade of retainers accompanying the bride as she is carried in a palanquin to her husband's home—are occasionally encountered in groves of Japanese cedar (*Cryptomeria japonica*), as they are represented here, usually when the sun shines through a rain shower.

(reverse illustrated)

14 *Inrō* with gong and striker

Lacquer over wood, three cases, of ovoid form
and section; *rōgin* surface, gold, brown, and black
hiramaki-e and *takamaki-e*, with scratched-detail
decoration; gold *nashiji* interiors; 3¾ x 2¾ x 1¼ in.
(9.5 x 7 x 3.2 cm); ca. 1865
Signature: *Zeshin* in scratched characters
Ojime: hardstone bead, with soft-metal fittings
Netsuke: lacquer over wood, *manju* type; *rōgin*
ground, decoration in colored *hiramaki-e* with
chestnuts, dull gold interior, en suite with the
inrō, signed: *Zeshin*
Published: Dunn (2001), pl. 72, p. 141

Zeshin, whose adoptive father was a maker of
bags and purses, was descended from a long line
of carpenters who specialized in ornamental
carving for temples. This gave him a familiarity
with Buddhist imagery, shown here by a temple
gong and padded striker. The dark silver-green
ground, the realistically pitted and slightly rusted
metal gong, the brown hanging cord on the reverse, and the green-tinged pad of the striker, all
demonstrate Zeshin's virtuosity in simulating a
variety of surfaces in lacquer. The minute areas
of scratched detail, used here to indicate the
leaves on sprays of orange blossom, are a characteristic of Zeshin's work.

An *inrō* with the same subject matter in the
Pfungst Bequest at the Victoria and Albert
Museum, London, forms part of Zeshin's famous
set of *inrō* representing the twelve months, which
can be confidently dated to 1865.[1] In this set the
gong-and-striker design provides the image for
the tenth month, when the gods of Buddhism and
Shintoism were summoned to the Great Shrine
at Izumo.[2] Orange blossom is traditionally associated with the tenth month, as are the chestnuts
on the en-suite netsuke.

1. See Earle, ed. (1986), no. 85, pp. 108–9. The storage box for
the set (now lost) was inscribed with this date.
2. Hutt (1997), p. 58. For a dispatch case decorated with the
same design, once owned by Kawanobe Itchō, the Kōami
school lacquerer, see Shioda, ed. (1908), n.p. (12th leaf from
the back, lower right). For a similar composition on an *inrō*,
see Meech (1995), no. 46, p. 96, an example with a natural
wood surface in the Weston Collection.

15 *Inrō* with ghost appearing over mosquito net

Lacquer over wood, four cases of rectangular form and oval section; black lacquer decorated in silver, gold, and multicolored *hiramaki-e*, black lacquer interior; 3¼ x 2¼ x ⅞ in. (8.3 x 5.7 x 2.22 cm); ca. 1860–90
Signature: *Zeshin* in scratched characters
Ojime: ivory, carved as a skull
Netsuke: lacquer, box type, decorated with a variety of ghosts and demons, signed *Kansai* (Koma Kansai II, 1766–1835)
Published: Honolulu Academy of Arts (1996), no. 68, pp. 156–57

A female ghost with blackened teeth looms over a mosquito net; the net extends to the reverse, where the specter's ethereal flame and a mosquito alighting on a paper lantern complete the image. Horror stories became very popular during the nineteenth century. Kabuki plays involving ghosts, in particular those by the playwright Tsuruya Nanboku IV (1755–1829), were often performed during the eighth month, when it was thought that they would induce chills down the spine as an antidote to the summer heat.

The subject is extremely unusual and may be unique in Zeshin's oeuvre. Technically, this *inrō* is a masterpiece, exploiting the lacquer medium to its maximum to convey the supernatural theme. It enjoyed some fame during the Meiji era. The print artist Utagawa Yoshiiku (1833–1904) included a copy of it, complete with a rendition of Zeshin's seal, in a series of *chūban*-size ghost prints published by Fukuda Kumajirō in 1890. The print in question is entitled *Amejo-jūroku*, which may be the name of Zeshin's spook.[1]

1. See Honolulu Academy of Arts (1996), no. 68, p. 156 for the print.

16 *Inrō* with water plantain and wood sorrel

Lacquer over wood, four cases, of squared form and oval section; decorated in gold, silver, and black lacquer, and *kanshitsu* (dry lacquer), with details in cut-gold and mother-of-pearl inlay, on a polished black ground, the interior of *nashiji* with *fundame* edges; with a design of water plantain (*omodaka*) on the front and wood sorrel (*katabami*) on the back; 3⅜ x 1⅞ x ⅞ in. (8.6 x 4.8 x 2.22 cm); ca. 1860–90
Signature: *Zeshin* in scratched characters
Ojime: coral bead
Netsuke: lacquer over wood, *manju*-type, en suite with the *inrō*, signed: *Zeshin*
Published: Bushell (1979), fig. 25, pp. 44–45[1]

This design, featuring water plantain (*Sagittaria trifolia*) and wood sorrel (*Oxalis japonica*), appears to have been one of Zeshin's favorites. It decorates a number of surviving *inrō*, netsuke, *tonkotsu*, and even writing boxes.

1. Bushell illustrates what is taken here to be the reverse of the *inrō* (see no. 9, n. 1), with a different netsuke, en suite with the wood sorrel design.

17 *Inrō* with autumn plants

Lacquer over wood, three cases, squared ovoid form and section; dark green lacquer with black raised decoration; 3⅛ x 2⅛ x ¾ in. (7.9 x 5.4 x 1.9 cm); ca. 1860–90
Signature: *Zeshin* in scratched characters
Netsuke: bamboo, *manju* type, decorated in lacquer with plants and open-scroll design, signed: *Taishin* [Ikeda Taishin]

Yamimaki-e—literally, an image that is in black lacquer on a very dark ground—was popular in the nineteenth century. It epitomizes a taste for designs that were elegant yet subdued, even to the point of being barely visible. This taste for restraint is one aspect of the concept of *iki*, of which Zeshin was a leading proponent.[1]

1. For a discussion of *iki*, see the Introduction.

18 *Inrō* with fireflies in a net

Lacquer over wood, five cases, of squared oval form and oval section; gold, silver, black, and red *hiramaki-e* and *takamaki-e*, with details in mother-of-pearl and pewter, on a dark green surface simulating patinated bronze, dull gold lacquer interior; 3 x 2¼ x ⅞ in. (7.6 x 5.7 x 2.22 cm); ca. 1860–90
Signature: *Zeshin* in scratched characters
Ojime: soft-metal of a bundle of bamboo twigs
Netsuke: box-type in colored lacquers of a firefly on bamboo, signed *Tomi* (Tomizo Saratani, b. 1949)

This design is a reference to Shain (Ch: Che Yin), an impoverished Chinese student of the Jin

dynasty (4th century A.D.), who devised a lantern made from a net full of fireflies to illuminate his night-time studies. Zeshin shows it here suspended from a bamboo pole on the front, with a broken wall on the back, emphasizing Shain's poverty-stricken circumstances.

Zeshin was fond of this composition, and several *inrō* employing it are recorded.[1]

1. For an example in the Khalili Collection, see Earle, ed. (1996), no. 49.

19 Netsuke of a toy sparrow

Lacquer over wood; gold, silver, and polished black decoration on a brown-green *seido-nuri* ground; 1½ x 1⅝ x ¾ in. (3.8 x 4.1 x 1.9 cm); ca. 1860–90
Signature: *Zeshin* in scratched characters
Published: Honolulu Academy of Arts (1996), no. 76, pp. 170–71

This charming netsuke of a tiny, stylized sparrow was originally made to be attached to a suitably themed *inrō*, now lost. On the back of the bird Zeshin has applied, with total abandon, an abstract decoration of flowering chrysanthemum and a triple-comma crest.

Edo-suzumi (Edo sparrows) was a slang term for the urban lower classes of Edo, whose tastes formed the cultural wellspring of Zeshin's art.

20 *Inrō* with Doll Festival figures behind a barred window

Lacquer over wood, three cases, squared oval form and section; decorated in various techniques on a polished gold ground; 3¼ x 2½ x ¾ in. (8.3 x 6.4 x 1.9 cm); ca. 1860–90
Signature: *Zeshin* in scratched characters
Ojime: lacquer bead
Netsuke: lacquer box-type, the lid in wood decorated with autumn grasses

Not only did Zeshin employ the theme of the Doll Festival (*Hina matsuri*), celebrated on the third day of the third month, repeatedly in painting, he also made a number of lacquer versions, including plaques, writing boxes, and parts of sets of boxes decorated with the theme of the Five Festivals (*Gosekku*). This is a rather unusual view of the subject, with the festival dolls displayed on tiers visible through a round, barred window, while a flowering plum tree appears on the back.

21 Tobacco container (*tonkotsu*) simulating a tea caddy

Lacquer over wood, with ivory cover; 2⅞ x 2⅞ x 1 in. (7.3 x 7.3 x 2.5 cm); ca. 1860–90
Signature: *Zeshin* in scratched characters
Ojime: lacquer bead
Netsuke: glazed stoneware and ivory, formed as a miniature tea-caddy

Zeshin was interested in the tea-drinking event, and studied under Yoshida Sōi, a tea master of the Sōhen school. During Zeshin's lifetime, the appreciation and drinking of powdered green tea was extremely fashionable, and the paraphernalia surrounding the occasion, such as ceramic tea caddies (*cha-ire*), flower vases (*hana-ire*), and fresh-water jars (*mizusashi*) from Bizen, Seto, Tamba, Takatori, and other kilns, became popular collectors' items. Zeshin's response was to revive an earlier technique for representing the surface of such ceramics, which he called *shūmon-nuri*, and which he achieved by brushing the wet lacquer with egg white and water so that it dried unevenly and resembled the appearance of these roughly formed wares.[1]

This *tonkotsu* is an excellent example of the type. Zeshin here not only mimics the body of a Seto or Tamba *cha-ire*, but also the lustrous brown and black glazes that often decorate these wares. Like his imitations of rosewood (see nos. 6, 7), a bronze dish (see no. 29), and Chinese ink-cakes (see no. 46-1, and nos. 10, 11), it is a trompe l'oeil masterpiece.

1. According to Earle, the technique of imitating ceramic surfaces in lacquer dates back at least to 1665, when a lacquer bowl representing Raku ware was reproduced in Simon Paulli's *Commentarius de abusu tabaci Americanorum veteri, et herbae theé Asiaticorum in Europa novo*; see Earle, ed. (1996), no. 61. See also Watson, ed. (1981), no. 157, pp. 247–48.

22 Set of Sword-Mounts (*koshirae*)

Lacquered wood and lacquer over wood; gold, silver, and black lacquer decoration; gold grips (*menuki*) formed as sparrows in flight, not by Zeshin; 16⅛ x 1½ x ¾ in. (41 x 3.8 x 1.9 cm); ca. 1860–90
Signature: *Zeshin* twice in scratched characters
Published: Honolulu Academy of Arts (1996), no. 77, pp. 172–73; Dunn (2001), pl. 76, p. 142

This set of sword-mounts for a dagger is an example of Zeshin's ability to transform everyday objects into works of great beauty. The wood of the scabbard has been purposely rusticated, with the natural pits and blemishes enhanced by carving, and then covered in a thin, clear lacquer. Colored lacquer has subsequently been applied to create the effect of a rotten branch under a trail of ivy. The ivy-leaf motif is continued on the lacquer mounts, which comprise a *fuchi-kashira*, *seppa*, *kojiri*, *kurikata*, *koiguchi,* and *kozuka* handle. They are decorated en suite in low relief in gold, black, and brown on a polished black ground, and offer a stylish contrast to the rough wood surface of the scabbard.

Zeshin made a number of sets of sword-mounts during his career. Approximately ten such sets are known; they were probably manufactured before 1876, when the wearing of swords in public was altogether proscribed. During the Edo period the ban had extended only to those below samurai status; by the nineteenth century, however, the rule had been corrupted, to judge from the large number of highly decorated and flamboyant dagger and short-sword mounts extant that would not have held much appeal for an austere samurai. On his sword-mounts Zeshin worked both alone or in conjunction with famous sword-fitting makers of the day, such as Kano Natsuo (1828–1898).

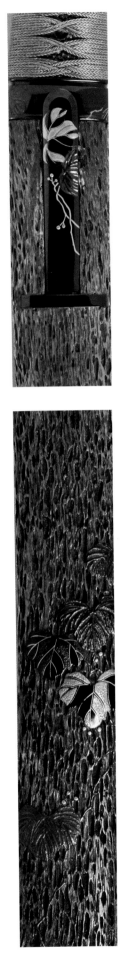

No. 22
Scabbard, detail
showing *kozuka*
handle (above
right); scabbard,
detail (below right)

23 Wood Sword (*bokutō*)

Lacquer over wood core simulating wood; decorated in lacquer and inlaid soft-metal; 17⅞ in. (45.4 cm) long; ca. 1860–90
Signature: *Zeshin* in scratched characters
Provenance: Ansei Tokubei
Exhibited: *Zeshin-ō Isaku Tenrankai* (Memorial exhibit of the work of Venerable Zeshin), Tokyo, 1908 (not in catalogue)
Published: Gōke (1981a), vol. 1, pl. 102; Dunn (2001), pl. 77, p. 142

During the Edo period medical doctors and those without samurai status were prohibited from bearing edged weapons, and a custom grew up for them to wear wood replicas (*bokutō*) of the short sword (*tantō*) carried by those of high social rank.

Waste lacquer has been worked to represent wood, the details of its grain and bark carefully rendered. The pair of grips (*menuki*) are of soft-metal: one is painted with lacquer to represent miniature kitchen utensils; the other is a votive picture featuring a rooster, perhaps a reference to the "Year of the Cock." The blade of the sword has been further embellished with a poem.

The inscription in gold lacquer is a *kyōka*, a form of witty verse in thirty-one syllables that enjoyed special popularity during the late eighteenth and early nineteenth centuries throughout Japan. Although the verse here is unsigned, it is a particularly well-known one by the Edo *kyōka* master Benbenkan Koryū (1756–1818). Along with being published in various anthologies, it was preserved for posterity by being carved into a memorial stone placed in the precincts of Jōenji, a Nichiren temple in the Nishi-Shinjuku district of Edo (modern-day Tokyo). The engraved stone was put in place the year after Benbenkan died and remains there to this day. The calligraphy of the inscription on the memorial stone is by the famous Edo poet, writer, and scholar Ōta Nanpo (Shokusanjin; 1749–1823). Both Benbenkan and Nanpo were members of the samurai class, but better remembered for their role in the Edo *kyōka* movement. It is not unreasonable to assume that Zeshin had actually seen the verse on this memorial stone, or had come across it in his reading. There are varying versions of the poem,

and in this rendition the character *meshi* (cooked rice) has been replaced with the character for *kome* (uncooked rice), though the meaning remains unchanged.

We can imagine that the ever-punctilious Zeshin, who constantly worked and reworked his lacquerware to get the exact effect he desired, would have been amused by the sentiment that if even things that we do regularly every day (such as cooking rice) do not turn out as expected, needless to say, when we encounter or do something new, we cannot hope for it to go as planned.

The poem reads:

sando taku	Even when we cook rice,
kome sae kowashi	Which we do three times a day,
yawarakashi	Sometimes it's too chewy,
omou mama ni wa	other times too soggy.
naranu yo no naka	Likewise in life, things don't always turn out
	Just the way we think they should.[1]

Zeshin's market was based on the urban culture of Edo, whose wealthy citizens did not necessarily have the status or inclination to wear swords in public; even if they did, carrying of swords was forbidden after 1876. It is not surprising, therefore, that a number of *bokutō* by Zeshin survive.[2] According to the inscription on the storage box, this example was once owned by Ansei Tokubei, a contemporary collector of Zeshin's work who lived in Yokohama.[3]

1. Taken from Gōke (1981a), vol. 1, p. 204, but note that the reading of the poem differs from the incorrect transcription he has of phrases in the second and third lines. Translation and commentary on the poem by John T. Carpenter.
2. See Shioda, ed. (1908), n.p. (9th leaf from the back), for two other examples.
3. A set of five paintings on the theme of the Five Festivals, a writing box, and a *tonkotsu* belonging to the same collector were all included in the 1908 memorial exhibition. The *bokutō* shown here is accompanied by a card listing it as an item in that exhibition. It does not, however, appear in the catalogue.

No. 23
Detail showing
poem

24 Cake Box (*kashibako*) with butter-flies and stylized chrysanthemums

Colored lacquer over wood; decorated in low
relief with gold and polished lacquer details;
4½ x 6⅝ x 2½ in. (11.4 x 16.8 x 6.4 cm); ca. 1860–90
Signature: *Zeshin* in scratched characters

The surface of this box and cover is lacquered to
simulate a russet iron container similar to those
produced by the Myōchin family of armor
makers. Zeshin called this surface *tetsusabi-nuri*.
Closely related to *seidō-nuri*, which simulated
patinated bronze, it was achieved much in the
same way. A mixture of charcoal dust, vinegar,
and iron-oxide dust was applied to the wet lacquer, which was then polished with different oils
and powders to create the desired effect.

The kidney shape of the box is one that Zeshin
often employed (see no. 28 for a smaller version).
Here the size and shape are reminiscent of a
rigid Chinese fan, a motif that, together with the
repoussé butterflies and polished lacquer chrysanthemum flowers, refers to Zhuang Zi (J: Sō Shi),
the ancient Chinese philosopher.[1] Zhuang posed
a famous question: after dreaming that he was a
butterfly, he awoke and could not decide whether
he was a butterfly dreaming that he was a man,
or the other way around. This paradox led him
to ponder the nature of human consciousness. In
the late Edo period, it became fashionable for
artists such as Zeshin to make *mitate-e*, images
that represented famous literary or historic scenes
viewed through a contemporary lens and included incongruous elements. Zeshin's use of the
ancient story here is an example of the diverse
sources that he drew on to layer his work with
meaning.

1. I am grateful to James Robinson, Curator of Asian Art at
the Indianapolis Museum of Art, for suggesting this subject.

25 Set of Stacked Boxes (*jūbako*) with willow and waterwheel

Lacquer over wood, rectangular form, five tiers, with two lids; black and green lacquer with gold *maki-e, kanshitsu*, dull silver, rust brown, polished black details, and mother-of-pearl and *harigaki* highlights; bright red interior; 16⅛ x 9 x 9⅝ in. (41 x 22.9 x 24.4 cm) overall; ca. 1860–90
Signature: *Zeshin* in scratched characters on the interior of each lid
Published: Dunn (2001), pl. 78, p. 142

Sets of five stacked food containers are the most spectacular of Zeshin's lacquer wares for domestic use. The Zeshin scholar Gōke Tadaomi illustrates four examples, three of which are in American collections,[1] and documents sixteen others, working from catalogues of exhibitions held between 1889 and 1940.[2] This may be the example listed under the name *Ryūsui yanagi maki-e jūbako* (Willow and flowing-water nest of lacquer boxes). The inscription on the storage box, signed *Kakan'an Chikushin*,[3] calls the set *Nami suisha shiki no hana* (Waves and waterwheel, flowers of the four seasons), a title not incompatible with that listed by Gōke, who was probably unfamiliar with the *jūbako* itself.

A stylized rural landscape is portrayed, in which a stream, with a willow tree and flowers of the four seasons on its banks, flows down through a steep-sided valley to a millpond and waterwheel at the base. Similar images decorate the two lids, one of which depicts a primitive wood irrigation system, the other the sails of the mill. The extra lid makes it possible to use this set of five trays

in various combinations. The bright red lacquer employed inside, customary for food boxes, provides a vivid contrast with the subdued tones on the exterior.

Competing techniques pioneered or reinvented by the master, such as the combed lacquer waves (*seigaha-nuri*) to represent flowing water and the dark green, patinated, bronzelike (*seidō-nuri*) river bank, are combined here in a virtuoso composition that unfolds fluently across the sides of the rectangular containers, marking this *jūbako* as a masterpiece. The contrasting surfaces, enhanced by shifts of scale and small, elaborate details, ensure a constant visual interest and play of light. The synthesizing of compositions based on earlier, Rinpa school lacquers and design manuals, such as works by Sakai Hōitsu (1761–1828) and the *Kōrin shinsen hyakuzu* (One hundred newly chosen designs by Kōrin) of 1864, with his own aesthetic and his extensive knowledge of lacquer surfaces, is characteristic of Zeshin's mature work.

1. Gōke (1981a), vol. 1, pls. 7–12, for examples in the Irving, Burke, and Haber collections.
2. Ibid., p. 199.
3. Shōji Chikushin (act. late 19th–early 20th century), a pupil of the master, was a very active certifier of Zeshin's works, and his inscriptions appear on a large number of storage boxes associated with them.

No. 25
Lid

No. 25
Alternate lid

26 Gourd Container

Lacquer over natural gourd, with gold and black lacquer decoration and mother-of-pearl highlights, the rim in simulated rosewood (*shitan-nuri*); 3¾ x 5¾ in. (9.5 x 14.6 cm); ca. 1860–90
Signature: *Zeshin* in gold lacquer

This natural gourd vessel, decorated with stylized flowers and rimmed with simulated Chinese rosewood, may have been used for burning incense.

27 Wine Cup (*sakazuki*) with camellia spray

Black, gold, and silver lacquer on horn; 1⅛ x 2½ in. (2.9 x 6.4 cm); ca. 1860–90
Signature: *Zeshin* in scratched characters
Provenance: Richard C. Bull
Published: Gōke (1981a), vol. 1, fig. 23 (b&w)

A spray of flowering camellia is lacquered in black, gold, and silver on one side of this horn sake cup. The cup is accompanied by a tightly woven basketry container with silver fittings (not illustrated), to enable the owner to suspend it from his waist.

28 Box (*hako*) with design of used nails

Dark green lacquer over leather; decorated in metallic color *hiramaki-e* and *takamaki-e*, pewter rim and rusticated paulownia wood lid; 3 x 4⅛ x 1⅝ in. (7.6 x 10.5 x 4.1 cm); ca. 1860–90
Signature: *Zeshin* in scratched characters
Published: Honolulu Academy of Arts (1996), no. 75, pp. 170–71

This small, kidney-shaped box (cf. no. 24) was probably made to hold tobacco, originally introduced into Japan from the New World when the Spanish came to trade in the Momoyama period. A container of the same shape and size exists in the O'Brien Collection in the Honolulu Academy of Art.[1] It also has a purposely distressed paulownia wood lid, which is decorated in gold and colored lacquer with loquats. The certification by Shōji Chikushin accompanying the O'Brien box suggests that it was made in 1870.

The present box is one of a small number of receptacles that Zeshin decorated with representations of twisted copper or iron nails.[2] Metal nails were valued and recycled in Edo-period Japan, and it was not until the Meiji era that a supply of straight nails was available through import. Zeshin's penchant for making designs from humble, everyday objects is a constant throughout his career. The nails are an element that may be associated with his family's traditional involvement with carpentry and temple sculpture.

1. Link (1979), no. 56, p. 121, ill. p. 131, who describes it as a sweetmeat box.
2. See Shioda, ed. (1908), n.p. (17th leaf from the back, lower register), for an *inrō*, once in the collection of Kaneda Kenjirō, who adopted Zeshin's daughter Sei. For two other examples, see Earle, ed. (1996), nos. 15 (sweetmeat container) and 65 (*inrō*).

29 Tray (*bon*) simulating pewter dish

Lacquer over wood; circular form, simulated
pewter surface; 8½ x 8½ x 1 in. (21.6 x 21.6 x 2.5
cm); ca. 1860–90
Signature: *Zeshin* in scratched characters

This is one of a number of trays made by Zeshin
to simulate metal dishes. They were intended for
serving small cakes or sweets during formal tea
gatherings, and appear to be based on the dishes
first introduced into Japan by the Portuguese and
Spanish in the late sixteenth century. Zeshin's
love of mimicking the surface and shape of an
object—the oxidized surface blemishes of the
dish are all carefully rendered—is fully realized
here. Another of these dishes, now in the possession of the English collector Edward (Ted)
Wrangham, excited the following comment by
Ernest Hart, the noted late nineteenth-century
Japanese art enthusiast and collector, to whom it
once belonged:

> Zeshin, one of the oldest, perhaps the last, of the
> lacquer workers of the old school of whose boxes
> and albums I have here some specimens. . . . Here
> is a plate made in the old style from the finest branch
> lac by Zeshin, and bearing his signature. You will
> see that he has, with infinite cunning, imitated the
> colour and patina of old bronze, and this plate is
> one which is particularly interesting as being per-
> haps the last work of the last worker of the good
> old school.[1]

1. Hart (1887), p. 23. For the dish itself, see Schaap, ed. (1987),
pl. 183, p. 62.

30 Tray (*bon*) with plovers in flight over waves

Green and black lacquer over wood; rectangular form with raised rim, green lacquer mimicking patinated bronze (*seidō-nuri*), the surface decorated with a combed-wave pattern and inlaid soft-metal details; 9½ x 6⅝ x ⅝ in. (24.1 x 16.8 x 1.59 cm); ca. 1860–90
Signature: *Zeshin* in scratched characters.

Although plovers flying above waves is an image that dates back to the fourteenth century, Zeshin's use of it here is another example of the influence of the Rinpa School of decorative design on his work. A great revival of interest in this style took place following the publication of the *Kōrin gafu* (The painting manual of Kōrin) by Nakamura Hōchū (act. late 18th–early 19th century) and other Rinpa design manuals in the nineteenth century. Updating this imagery and combining it with newly revived lacquer techniques allowed Zeshin to achieve compositions that were both modern and familiar in their appeal. He employed the plover motif on large works, such as his set of stacking food containers featuring loaded grain carriers sailing down a river, now in the Irving Collection, New York,[1] and also on small, personal lacquerwares, such as *inrō* and the tray shown here.

1. Watt and Ford (1991), no. 144, pp. 284–85.

31 Tray (*bon*) with plovers in flight above a reinforced river bank

Lacquer over wood; rectangular form with raised rim, decorated in various techniques, with gold, silver, and colored lacquer details, and inlaid mother-of-pearl highlights; 16¼ x 8½ x 1½ in. (41.3 x 21.6 x 3.8 cm); ca. 1860–90
Signature: *Zeshin* in scratched characters

The flight of plovers above a shoreline is rendered here in a gold-on-black lacquer decoration that is reminiscent of a fifteenth-century lacquer type of decoration that featured a very stylized drawing of these birds. By the seventeenth century flights of the birds, sometimes in tandem with drying fishing nets, can be found pictured on a number of lacquers made for domestic use, including incense burners and writing and document boxes.[1] Here the image is deployed with water rendered in Zeshin's newly revived combed-wave technique, with dry lacquer and scratched details, and demonstrates the artist's skill at seamlessly combining new and old imagery and techniques to make stylish modern artifacts.

1. For a fifteenth-century example of this bird motif on an incense burner in the Cleveland Museum, see Yamane (1981), pl. 7.

32 Tray (*bon*) with bats in flight above a stream

Rectangular form with raised edge; cypress wood decorated in gold and silver lacquer; 10⅛ x 9⅛ in. (26.4 x 23.8 cm); ca. 1860–90
Signature: *Hoko zu Zeshin sha* (Copied from an old design by Zeshin) in black lacquer
Published: Gōke (1981a), vol. 1, pl. 53

Of all the works in the Edson Collection, this wood tray most betrays Zeshin's fondness for Rinpa school imagery and design. The painter Sakai Hōitsu (1761–1828), who had made a personal study of the work of the Kyoto artist and lacquerer Ogata Kōrin (1658–1716), was the first to coin the name of the school, taking the *Rin* character of Kōrin and combining it with the *Ha* for "family." In 1815, to mark the hundredth anniversary of Kōrin's death, Hōitsu published the woodblock-illustrated catalogue *Kōrin hyakuzu* (One hundred works by Kōrin), which was intended to bring about a revival of Kōrin's painting style and proved to be very successful. Hōitsu's studies also revealed that the sources of Kōrin's imagery were Hon'ami Kōetsu (1558–1637) and Tawaraya Sōtatsu (act. ca. 1600–1640). The efforts that Hōitsu and his followers made to popularize the school were such that Kōrin's decorative style, which combined forceful abstract design with a keen observation of nature, and flattened compositions and patterning with evenly applied solid colors, was disseminated throughout Japan and became highly influential.

In lacquer, Zeshin's response to this vogue was to make numerous small *inrō* in the Kōrin manner, mimicking his style of slightly dull lacquer and inlaid mother-of-pearl decoration to such a degree that, were it not for the signature, they would be difficult to distinguish from Kōrin's work. Zeshin also made direct copies, for example, a writing box in 1863, after one by Kōrin that depicted the medieval courtier Ariwara no Narihira on a fan; this box once belonged to Koma Kansai II and is now in the possession of the Nezu Institute of Fine Arts, Tokyo.[1] Such copies were part of Zeshin's extensive research beginning in the 1840s on earlier lacquer masters.

In the present tray the stylized eddies of water owe a clear debt to Kōrin, while the bats, symbols of good fortune, and their clover-leaf decoration are Zeshin's own. Zeshin's signature acknowledges his composition as copied from an earlier work.

1. See Gōke (1981a), p. 168.

33 Tray (*bon*) with budding lotus

Lacquer over wood; rectangular form with raised
edges, decorated in black and gold *shishiaimaki-e* on a dark green *seido-nuri* ground; 13⅝ x
8 x 1⅛ in. (34.6 x 20.3 x 2.9 cm); ca. 1860–90
Signature: *Zeshin* in scratched characters

Traditionally associated with Buddhism, the lotus
is a flower symbolizing enlightenment and men-
tal purity. This tray was probably made for use on
a family altar to hold votive implements.

34 Set of Dining Vessels in Kasuga Shrine style

Comprising: tray (*bon*): lacquer over wood, rectangular with raised rim and foot, decorated in black and red lacquer, with mother-of-pearl inlay of butterflies; 13 x 17½ x 2¼ in. (33 x 44.5 x 7 cm); ewer (*heishi*): black lacquer over wood, gold decoration of leaves and pairs of cranes; 6 x 4½ in. (15.2 x 11.4 cm); three-tiered food container and lid (*jūbako*): black lacquer over wood with gold decoration of cranes and leaves; 7⅝ x 6 x 6⅜ in. (19.4 x 15.2 x 16.2 cm); sake cup (*sakazuki*): lacquer over wood; circular form on raised cylindrical foot, in black lacquer on red ground with a crow in flight; ¼ x 3⅝ in. (1.9 x 9.2 cm); sake cupstand (*heidai*): tapered cylindrical form surmounted by a tray, black lacquer over wood with gold decoration of leaves; 1883
Signature: *Koma Zeshin sha* (tray); *Gyōnen nanajūnanasai ō Zeshin* (Venerable Zeshin at the age of seventy-seven) (sake cup) in lacquer

According to the inscriptions on the inside of the *jūbako* lid, the underside of the tray, and on the storage boxes, all in Zeshin's hand, this set of dining vessels was copied from one in the collection of the Kasuga Shrine of Nara. From the appearance of the decoration, the original set was probably employed for the entertainment of important guests and may have dated from as early as the seventeenth century. The decoration, in gold on black, is typical of lacquers of that date.

The Kasuga Shrine was founded in the eighth century by the influential Fujiwara family. It is located at the foot of Mount Mikasa and is one of the most important shrines of the Nara area. The structure is rebuilt every twenty years in accordance with Shinto beliefs. It would have been one of the places that Zeshin visited on his journey to the Nara district in the 1830s and again in 1875, when he went to study the objects from the imperial collection in the Shōsōin Repository. Zeshin made a number of paintings of its grounds, famous for their stone lanterns, maple trees, and wandering deer (see no. 46-7).

It seems apparent that Zeshin did not have a complete set to work from. The sake cup in particular, with its black crow on a red ground, appears to be in Zeshin's own style and was probably added to replace a lost piece. The inlaid mother-of-pearl insects on the tray, like the rotting leaves in no. 1 and falling fruit in no. 4, add a humorous note to what is generally a very conservative piece.

Lid interior inscribed *Kasuga Jinja Sanmai bon maki e* (Three tier set of trays from Kasuga Shrine) signed *Koma Zeshin bo* (copied) and with *kakikan*

Pages 82 and 83: Tray detail and sake cup

PAINTING

Paintings in Ink and Color

Zeshin's interest in painting began in 1822 when he was advised by his master Koma Kansai II to improve his compositional skills. He chose to take classes under Suzuki Nanrei (1775–1844), a popular local artist who had studied the fashionable Shijō style with Watanabe Nangaku (1763–1813), one of Maruyama Ōkyo's most talented students.[1] As with his lacquer works, very little of Zeshin's painting output can be securely dated to the Edo period. This stage of his life seems to have been more devoted to study and development, and many paintings he made at the time appear to have been lost, making an evaluation of his early career difficult. This was the period when he achieved success, however, and he was then better known for his paintings than for his lacquerwares. He won several commissions for large, spectacular works, such as his votive pictures preserved in various shrines and temples in Tokyo, and his suite of sliding doors housed in the Daiyōin, a temple in Kyoto. These, while not now in good condition, give us an idea of his drawing style and sense of composition. His fan paintings, ephemera as they were, have largely been used and discarded. His small-scale book illustrations, because the printed images were mass produced, have survived and reveal his strength of line and his capacity to create visual surprises, which is also a feature of his lacquer work.

Like many painters of the nineteenth century, Zeshin was eclectic in his sources. He would have been exposed to traditional styles as he grew up, and soon after becoming a lacquer apprentice began to study the fashionable, "uninhibited" Maruyama-Shijō manner under Nanrei. Once he went to Kyoto in 1830 to study with Okamoto Toyohiko, he was exposed not only to the Maruyama School, but also to the works of the closely related Nanga, or literati, school, founded by Yosa Buson (1716–1783) and Ike Taiga (1723–1776).

We can also look at his Edo period images through his contributions to illustrated books and his prints. Zeshin was a prolific printmaker, mainly in the form of Shijō-style *surimono*, or privately published greeting cards and announcements. His friendship with Utagawa Kuniyoshi (1797–1861), a leading ukiyo-e artist of the "floating world," brought him into contact with the huge Edo publishing industry that supported printmakers of the Ukiyo-e School. Kuniyoshi is thought, despite being the older of the two men, to have been Zeshin's first student, taking painting lessons in the Shijō style with him in order to broaden his own visual repertoire, under the name Senshin. Zeshin made several joint works with Kuniyoshi and with Kuniyoshi's students.[2]

In contrast to the small number of paintings extant from the Edo period, large numbers of Zeshin's paintings from the Meiji era have survived. These range in style from Maruyama-Shijō works derived from his teachers in both Edo and Kyoto, *bunjinga* (literati paintings) in the style of Yosa Buson from the same source, Rinpa School decorative painting, Chinese landscape painting in the Northern Song manner favored by such leading artists as Tani Banchō (1763–1840), early Ukiyo-e school painting derived from Zeshin's studies of the so-called Hikone Screens in Hikone

Castle owned by Ii Naosuke (1815–1860), formal Tosa and Kano school works, in addition to traditional Japanese painting styles known as *yamato-e*.

With such a wide repertoire of styles available to him, Zeshin applied himself to the production of scrolls, albums, screens, and prints, working very much as the head of a large professional studio. His subject matter includes: landscape, both large, formal works and small, intimate paintings, which betray a love and sympathy for the natural world around him; nature studies; portraits; traditional images made for New Year and to mark major festivals; and paintings designed to engender patriotic sentiments among their viewers. His skill was such that he could fluidly mix styles, painting part of a composition in one manner and including elements of another to add variety.

As the fourth-generation head of the Shijō school, Zeshin was the leader of a group of these painters employed to decorate the Hama Rikyu Palace, where Emperor Meiji entertained official guests, among them, in 1879, President Grant. The palace was later destroyed during the great earthquake of 1923.

Paintings in Lacquer

Painting in lacquer was not a technique invented by Zeshin—other artists had previously worked in the medium—but Zeshin applied his knowledge of lacquer to develop the technique significantly, enabling him to apply it in a wide variety of formats. By overlaying thin coats of lacquer and mixing in different ingredients, he could achieve a tangible thickness to the pigment which allowed portrayal in the round, while retaining enough resilience to permit a scroll so painted to be rolled and unrolled without flaking. These images, usually on paper, were known as *urushi-e* (lacquer painting), not to be confused with framed lacquer (*maki-e*) panels designed to have the appearance of Western oil paintings and to be similarly hung.[3]

Although the new *urushi-e* technique allowed Zeshin to use traditional methods to achieve realistic results, the process was exacting and difficult to master. Color pigments had to be mixed in with the lacquer, restricting the palette that could be employed. Such was Zeshin's skill that despite the viscous quality of lacquer, his line appears spontaneous, free, and full of vigorous movement. Imitations by his students, of which there are many, never have this free-flowing quality. The technique did not survive long after Zeshin's death in 1891.

Zeshin employed the *urushi-e* technique on all sizes of work, including folding screens and large panels, hanging scrolls, and small pictorial albums. These albums appear to have been of two types. Those in the first group issued in Zeshin's lifetime are usually in the *shikishiban* (rectangular poetry paper) format; they were originally conceived of as sets of not necessarily related images, often featuring plant and animal studies, with the occasional landscape and still-life, which were then mounted into albums to be sold. One such album is in the Imperial Household Collection, purchased at the National Industrial Exposition (Naikoku kangyō hakurankai) in 1881;[4] the signature on one of its images (*painted at the age of seventy-five*) indicates that Zeshin completed the paintings in the same year. Number 46 in the Edson collection belongs to this group. Originally it appears to have consisted of seven images; it retains the paper wrapper inscribed in the artist's handwriting with this figure, suggesting that it might have been issued by Zeshin as an unbound set. Another image could then have been added when the paintings were presented as they now are, mounted as an album, probably in the late 1920s.

In his lacquer-painting albums Zeshin frequently applies the Maruyama school tenet of realistic observation (*shasei*), often including detailed drawings and preparatory studies featuring insects, amphibians, or animals (see no. 45-16 for studies of flying insects and no. 46-4 for the study of a mottled toad). Zeshin also frequently records his debt to Maruyama Ōkyo, stating that the composition was either after Ōkyo or derived from a work by him (see nos. 44-32 and 46-2).

The other type of album consists of lacquer sketches that were assembled by Zeshin's students after his death in 1891. This would explain the difference in dates sometimes found in the same album.

Zeshin, like many Japanese professional artists, often repeated the same or similar images in his compositions. The deer in no. 46-7, for example, pictured beside one of the red lanterns of the Kasuga Shrine in Nara, appears in other albums, as do some of the landscapes and nature studies. Unfortunately, because of the commercial popularity of these works, numbers of albums have been broken up and the separated sheets remounted as hanging scrolls (for example, no. 47).

The collection of lacquer paintings by Zeshin in the Edson Collection is particularly distinguished, and features, in hanging scrolls and albums, nearly all the techniques that Zeshin employed.

1. Fould (1979), p. 20.
2. An example is a large *surimono* datable to 1849 depicting an album open to show two pages with a portrait of the actor Ichikawa Ebizō V as Sōjōbō, the king of the Tengu on the right, and his son Ichikawa Danjūrō VIII as Ushiwaka on the left, set on a background decorated with a design of a gourd in flower and a writing brush in a case. The album is signed by Kuniyoshi, the background by Zeshin. See Hillier (1979), no. 319.
3. For Zeshin's *maki-e*, which often became prize-winning entries in national and international expositions, see Gōke (1981a), vol. 1, pls. 116–120; Earle, ed. (1996), pp. 28–30, nos. 27–30.
4. See Yonemura et al. (1997), no. 56, pp. 182–83 (entry by Ohkuma Toshiyuki).

35 Doll Festival Figures

Hanging scroll, ink and color on silk; image size
13⅞ x 17¼ in. (35.2 x 43.8 cm), overall size 50 x
22¼ in. (127 x 56.5 cm); ca. 1860–90
Signature: *Zeshin* and sealed *Shin*

The five main festivals and their associated images provided artists such as Zeshin with numerous commissions, for it was traditional to hang paintings related to the calendar. This image of a pair of dolls—an emperor and his empress in traditional Heian-period robes— would have been hung to celebrate the Doll Festival, held by households on the third day of the third month to pray for the health and happiness of daughters. Zeshin appears to have had a particular fondness for this subject, and many examples of Doll Festival images by him, seen in a variety of contexts, are extant (see nos. 19, 48).

During the nineteenth century, it became fashionable to render the mounts of a hanging scroll in paint rather than actually mounting the image on silk in the traditional way. Zeshin was particularly skilled in this regard and was capable of mimicking a wide range of fabrics and styles of mounting. Zeshin also became famous for making paintings of hanging scrolls in which the figures in the image literally seem to jump out of their confines onto the fictive mounts. The results are playful essays in trompe l'oeil.[1]

Here the artist has chosen different patterns to represent the various parts of the mount. The strips above and below the painting (*ichimonji*) and the two strips hanging down (*fūtai*) are rendered in white, gold, and silver with a design of seashells; the inner mounts (*chūmawashi*) are in gold pigment on purple, with birds flying amid cloud-bestrewn willows and flowering trees; and the top and bottom panels (*tenchi*) are patterned with an abstract scrolling motif in purple on gray. This custom of painting the mounts was taken up by Zeshin's students and followers and can be seen in other hanging scrolls in the Edson Collection (see nos. 37, 52).

1. See Gōke (1981a), nos. 249, 263, 267.

36 *Rocks and Waterfall*

Hanging scroll, ink and light color on silk; 68 x
28 in. (172.7 x 71.1 cm); 1889
Signature: *Tairyūkyo Zeshin* and sealed *Koma*

By the 1880s, Zeshin had emerged as a leader
of the Maruyama-Shijō school, and it was as the
fourth hereditary master that he participated in
the interior decoration of the newly constructed
Imperial palace in 1886. According to Imperial
Household records, Zeshin was responsible for a
four-panel sliding door decorated with herons
and hollyhocks, with irises on the reverse.[1]

For Zeshin, Maruyama Ōkyo was a source of
inspiration throughout his career, a fact to which
he often referred when signing a painting (see
no. 46-2). Ōkyo had made waterfalls something
of a specialty, and his renderings of this traditional subject demonstrate how he combined his
own revolutionary pictorial approach with long-
established themes (see Introduction, fig. 2).
Unlike his predecessors, Ōkyo de-emphasized
the fall of water by moving the viewer's vantage
point closer, drawing attention to the water
churning through the rocks at the base, a treatment that Zeshin follows here. Like Ōkyo,
Zeshin made a large number of waterfall paintings, many dating from his later years, and
numerous examples survive.[2]

1. Fould (1979), p. 24. For the screens, see Gōke (1981a), vol. 1,
pls. 216–18.
2. The storage box for this scroll, signed by Zeshin himself,
gives his age as eighty-three, indicating that it was done in
1889. For other examples of Zeshin's treatment of waterfalls,
see nos. 3, 4; Shioda, ed. (1908), 51st leaf from the front; and
Gōke (1981a), vol. 1, pls. 242–44, 255, 256.

37 *Willow Tit Perched above a Waterfall*

Hanging scroll, ink and color on silk; 36½ x 13⅛
in. (92.7 x 33.3 cm); ca. 1885–90
Signature: *Tairyūkyo Zeshin* and sealed *Tairyūkyo*

This variant of Zeshin's favorite waterfall scene
(see no. 36) has been given a trompe l'oeil mounting showing maple trees in autumn by his student
Shōji Chikushin at the age of eighty-one, according to the inscription on the lower left. The storage box certification by Chikushin's follower
Hōshin (act. first half of the 20th century), who
contributed the lacquer roller-ends (*jiku*), states
that Chikushin painted the mount in Showa 9
(1934). It is an example of the efforts made by
Zeshin's descendants to market his works long
after the master's death.

38 *A Hawk Glaring at Its Reflection in a Waterfall*

Pair of hanging scrolls, ink and light color on silk; each 56½ x 10¾ in. (143.5 x 27.3 cm); 1881
Signature: *Zeshin sha* and *Gyōnen nanajūgo-ō* (at the age of seventy-five) *Zeshin*, both sealed *Tairyūkyo*

Zeshin painted more than one version of this scene, depicting a hawk on its nest protecting its young from its own reflection in the waterfall opposite. A larger version is in the Museum für Kunst und Gewerbe, Hamburg.[1]

1. See Yamane Yūzō et al., ed. (1980), vol. 6, pls. 112, 113.

39 *Tiger in Snow*

Hanging scroll, ink on silk; 49¼ x 23¾ in. (125.1 x 60.3 cm); 1888
Signature: *Gyōnen hachijūni sei* (at the age of eighty-two) *Zeshin* and sealed *Shin*

Zeshin made a number of paintings of tigers towards the end of his life. In doing so he was exercising his traditionalist credentials. The vigorous brushwork that he employed in these images owed nothing to the contemporary Meiji-era ideas of Westernization, but rather harked back to a line of Far Eastern painting which dated from ancient times. In Asia the tiger has always represented cunning and martial valor.

Although often formulaic in their depiction of the animal's fur and stripes, Zeshin's renderings demonstrate his efforts to keep the Maruyama-Shijō school vital, and also show a complete mastery of traditional ink painting, often adding lacquer to intensify the black tones of the image. The tiger here is seen looking out from his lair, partly screened by an overhang of snow; the only vegetation visible is snow-covered bamboo, the plant with which tigers are normally paired in Asian iconography.

40 *Entrance to a Country Temple in Autumn*

Hanging scroll, ink and color on silk; 36½ x
13⅛ in. (92.7 x 33.3 cm); ca. 1860–90
Signature: *Zeshin* and sealed *Tairyūkyo*

Many of Zeshin's paintings and lacquerwares
present images of the countryside. These views
display a romantic sensitivity on Zeshin's part,
and a fondness for the innocence of life in rural
Japan. They also reflect Zeshin's interest in the
poetry of Bashō and his followers (see no. 6),
who revered the beauty of the Japanese landscape
and the simplicity of country life. Here a slightly
dilapidated gate of a temple, guarded by figures
of the Deva kings, is typical of the scenes that
caught Zeshin's eye in his landscape painting.

41 *Kakushigi and His Family*

Hanging scroll, ink, color, and gold pigment on silk; 48⅝ x 27⅞ in. (123.5 x 70.8 cm); ca. 1880–90
Signature: *Tairyūkyo Zeshin* and one artist's seal (unread)
Published: Shibata (1912), n.p. (29th leaf from the front); Gōke (1981b), p. 167

This colorful painting in the Chinese mode portrays the celebrated Tang general Kakushigi (Ch. Guo Ziyi; 697–781), with his family in attendance. Kakushigi served loyally and tirelessly under four successive emperors. For thirty troubled years, he led the Chinese army on several Central Asian campaigns and then crushed the An Lushan rebellion of 755–63. Miraculously surviving his many battles and court intrigues, Kakushigi lived to the advanced age of eighty-four and was lavishly rewarded by his grateful rulers.

Zeshin represents the old man enthroned in his palace with his sons, daughters, and grandchildren in attendance. He had eight sons and seven sons-in-law, all of whom rose to prominent government positions. Their offspring were so numerous that he could not recognize half of them when they came to pay their respects, and could only bow to them in greeting when they stood before him.

This finely painted work, set on a terrace opening to the outside, employs typical Zeshin flourishes; the landscape painting on the throne behind the general, for example, and the detailed depiction of the lacquer and ceramic vessels on the table beside it and of the textiles worn by visiting family members. The rockwork and grasses in the lower right are also typical of his painting style.

Zeshin derived his subject from Ōkyo's famous set of screens on this theme for the Daijōji Temple in Kasumi, Hyōgo Prefecture. The figure of Kakushigi was fashionable among the merchant classes as a symbol of longevity, wealth, fertility, and marital harmony. It was for this reason that Zeshin included the subject in the set of screens he made for the altar room of the Daiyūin Temple in Kyoto early in his career.[1] During the Meiji era, Kakushigi became an exemplar of loyalty to the emperor, a patriotic sentiment very popular at the time.

Celebrated in Zeshin's lifetime, this painting was included in the second memorial exhibition organized by the Committee for the Exhibition of Works by the Venerable Zeshin.

1. See Gōke (1981a), vol. 1, pl. 224.

42 *Mount Hōrai*

Hanging scroll, ink and color on silk; 66 ¾ x 18 in.
(169.5 x 45.7 cm); 1881
Signed: *Nanajūgosai* (at the age of seventy-five)
Zeshin and sealed *Zeshin*
Published: Shioda, ed. (1908), n.p. (52nd leaf from
the front)

Mount Hōrai, or Hōrai-san, is the Japanese trans-
literation of the Chinese place name Penglai-shan.
Daoists believed Penglai to be an island paradise
in the Eastern Sea, or Sea of Japan. The island
was said to be inhabited by Immortals, together
with various animals and birds associated with
longevity, such as deer, cranes, and long-haired
turtles.

From the late Heian period images related to
Mount Hōrai were used on bronze mirrors, especially those given as marriage gifts among the no-
bility. By the Edo period, these auspicious motifs
were widely used at every level of society. Paintings of them were popular, and Zeshin made a
number of different versions of the subject, especially towards the end of his career.

Here Zeshin depicts the craggy, pine-covered
rocks of the island rising from a mist-shrouded
sea. A pair of cranes is perched on the rocks
above the trees, and the New Year's sun rises in
the distance.

43 *Bird and a Flowering Vine*

Four sliding panels, ink, color and gold wash on
silk, with metal fittings; each 7½ x 6¼ in. (19.1 x
15.9 cm); 1879
Signature: *Jinen nanajūsan* (at the age of seventy-
three) *Zeshin sha*, and sealed *Tairyūkyo*

A small brown and white bird is shown in flight
beside a branch of *Kazura japonica*, a tree-climb-
ing plant which flowers between June and Sep-
tember. In Japan, where its viscous sap was used
during the Edo period by men as pomade, it was
known colloquially as *binan kazura*, or "climber
of handsome men."

These sliding panels were once part of a larger
suite of furniture fittings, which have now been
lost. They were sold, as is, at the Tokyo Art Dealers Association in 1931.[1] Zeshin completed a number of commissions to decorate interiors, most of
which have been destroyed or dismantled in the
intervening years. His most notable commission
was the interior of the Enryōkan, part of the
Hama Rikyū Palace, where Emperor Meiji entertained official guests, which fell victim to the
great Kantō earthquake of 1923.

1. Sasaki and Sasaki (2004), no. 149, p. 36.

時年七十三
老真写

44 Miniature album of forty-six leaves

Cover: woven silk brocade; calligraphic title
page, ink on gold leaf; the remaining leaves
mounted with forty-five images, lacquer on
paper or lacquer on gold leaf; each 2 x 2½ in.
(5.1 x 6.4 cm); ca. 1881
Each signed and sealed variously
For additional images in black and white,
see Appendix

1 Title page in calligraphy: *Raku* (for fun)
Signature: *Koma Zeshin* and sealed *Koma*

2 *Crow and New Year's Sun*
Signature: *Zeshin* and sealed *Ze*

3 *Flowering Plum*
Signature: *Zeshin* and sealed *Shin*

4 *Pestle, Mortar, and Herbs*
Signature: *Zeshin* and sealed *Shin*

5 *Young Ferns*
Signature: *Zeshin* and sealed *Shin*

6 *Fuji from Mihō*
Signature: *Zeshin* and sealed *Ze*

7 *Plovers and Waves*
Signature: *Zeshin* and sealed *Shin*

8 *Horse and Cherry Blossoms*
Signature: *Zeshin* and sealed *Shin*

9 *Cat and Butterfly*
Signature: *Zeshin* and sealed *Shin*

10 *Swimming Fish*
Signature: *Zeshin* and sealed *Shin*

11 *Bamboo Shoots*
Signature: *Zeshin* and sealed *Ze*

12 *Gourd Vine*
Signature: *Zeshin* and sealed *Shin*

No. 44-18

No. 44-22

13 *Flat Fish*
Signature: *Zeshin* and sealed *Shin*

14 *Insect on Lotus Pond*
Signature: *Zeshin* and sealed *Shin*

15 *Rock and Gnarled Tree*
Signature: *Zeshin* and sealed *Shin*

16 *Carp*
Signature: *Zeshin* and sealed *Shin*

17 *Peony in Rainstorm*
Signature: *Zeshin* and sealed *Shin*

18 *Persimmon, Pears, Melons, and Ants*
Signature: *Zeshin* and sealed *Shin*

19 *River Embankment and Fish Leaping*
Signature: *Zeshin* and sealed *Ze*

20 *Bamboo in Rain*
Signature: *Zeshin* and sealed *Shin*

21 *Rocks and Shells on Beach*
Signature: *Zeshin* and sealed *Ze*

22 *Octopus and Seaweed*
Signature: *Zeshin* and sealed *Shin*

23 *Squirrels Gathering Nuts*
Signature: *Meiji kanoto mi shūjitsu* (On an autumn
day in the Snake year of Meiji [1881]), *Zeshin* and
with *kakihan*

24 *Momotarō Emerging from a Peach*
Signature: *Zeshin* and sealed *Ze*

25 *Puppies and Broken Umbrella*
Signature: *Zeshin* and sealed *Ze*

26 *Flowering Rose and Rockwork*
Signature: *Zeshin nanajūgo-o* (at the age of
seventy-five) and sealed *Shin*

27 *Hanging Gourd Vine*
Signature: *Zeshin* and sealed *Shin*

28 *Tadpoles*
     Signature: *Meiji jūyon kanoto mi shūjitsu sha*
     (Copied on an autumn day in the Snake year,
     Meiji 14 [1881]), *Zeshin* and sealed *Moku*

29 *Chestnuts*
     Signature: *Zeshin* and sealed *Shin*

30 *Rabbit beneath the Moon*
     Signature: *Zeshin* and sealed *Shin*

31 *Coastal Landscape*
     Signature: *Zeshin* and sealed *Shin*

32 *Chestnuts in a Basket*
     Inscribed: *Ōkyo*; signature: *Zeshin utsutsu* (copied)
     and sealed *Moku*

33 *Autumn Flowers*
     Signature: *Zeshin* and sealed *Shin*

34 *Mount Fuji from the Foothills*
     Signature: *Zeshin* and sealed *Shin*

35 Matsutake *Mushrooms*
     Signature: *Tairyūkyo Zeshin* and sealed *Shin*

36 *Frogs Wrestling*
     Signature: *Zeshin* and sealed *Zeshin*

37 *Seagulls and Drying Fishing Nets*
     Signature: *Zeshin* and sealed *Shin*

38 Reishi *Fungus in a Jar, Miniature Rock
     Garden in a Bowl*
     Signature: *Zeshin* and sealed *Shin*

39 *Sacred Cryptomeria Tree and Gates*
     Signature: *Zeshin* and sealed *Shin*

40 *Egret Wading in a Stream*
     Signature: *Zeshin* and sealed *Shin*

41 *Two Mice and Daikoku's Hammer*
     Signature: *Zeshin* and sealed *Shin*

42 *Bamboo*
     Signature: *Zeshin* and sealed *Shin*

No. 44-32

No. 44-36

43 *Homing Geese and the Moon*
    Signature: *Zeshin* and sealed *Shin*

44 *Flowering Iris in a Bucket*
    Signature: *Zeshin* and sealed *Shin*

45 *Fishing Village in a Cove*
    Signature: *Zeshin* and sealed *Shin*

46 *Mount Fuji above Drying Fishing Nets*
    Signature: *Hachijūissai* (at the age of eighty-one)
    Zeshin and sealed *Shin*

No. 45-5

45 Album of twenty lacquer paintings

Cover: woven silk, with gold-leaf title slip; twenty
paintings, lacquer on paper or gold leaf, each 3½
x 4⅜ in. (8.9 x 11.1 cm); ca. 1885
Each signed and sealed variously
For additional images in black and white,
see Appendix

1 *Dragon in Clouds*
Signature: *Koma Zeshin sei* and sealed *Ze*

2 *Bird on Willow Branch*
Signature: *Zeshin* and sealed *Shin*

3 *Flower Cart*
Signature: *Zeshin* and sealed *Zeshin*

4 *Cryptomeria Tree and Mount Fuji*
Signature: *Zeshin* and sealed *Zeshin*

5 *Weeping Cherry Tree behind Fence*
Signature: *Zeshin* and sealed *Shin*

6 *Daikoku's Hammer and Bag of Treasure*
Signature: *Zeshin* and sealed *Zeshin*

7 *Leaping Carp*
Signature: *Zeshin* and sealed *Moku*

No. 45-9

18 *Butterflies and Shaded Chrysanthemums*
    Signature: *Zeshin* and sealed *Shin*

19 *Farmer Crossing Bridge in Winter*
    Signature: *Zeshin* and sealed *Shin*

20 *Mount Fuji*
    Signature: *Tairyūkyo Zeshin* and sealed *Shin*

No. 45-16

No. 45-17

No. 46-3

46 Album of eight leaves

Cover: woven silk with soft-metal fittings; leaves
mounted with eight paintings, lacquer on paper
or gold leaf; each 7½ x 6⅛ in. (19.1 x 17.5 cm);
ca. 1880–90
Each signed and sealed variously

1 *Horsefly on Ink-Cake, Paper-Wrapped Ink Stick*
Signature: *Tairyūkyo Zeshin sha* and sealed *Koma*
(illustration on page 17)

2 *Finch Pecking at Seeds*
Signature: *Ōkyo ishitsu sha* (Copied in lacquer after
Ōkyo) *Zeshin* and sealed *Zeshin*

No. 46-4

3 *Cat Scratching Its Ear*
  Signature: *Zeshin* and sealed *Koma*

Zeshin made repeated versions of this image in many different formats.

4 *Mottled Toad*
  Signature: *Zeshin* and sealed *Shin*

The original watercolor drawing for this image is in the Tokyo National University of Fine Arts and Music Collection (Yokomizo and Satsuma [2005], p. 314). Zeshin's use of lacquer here enabled him to capture the almost three-dimensional quality of the reptile's mottled and leathery skin more successfully than in watercolor.

5 *Terrapin Falling Backwards into Water*
  Signature: *Zeshin* and sealed *Tairyūkyo*

Zeshin's studio was on the bank of a river, giving
him plenty of opportunity to observe nature and
record events in the everyday life of its denizens.

No. 46-6

6 *Flowering Plant*
   Signature: *Zeshin* and sealed *Koma*

A species of hibiscus is shown in flower. Such
was Zeshin's mastery of the lacquer medium that
he was able to convey the almost feathery light-
ness of the petals in contrast to the plant's stiff
stalk and prominent, almost ungainly lobed leaves.

No. 46-8

7 *Deer and Lantern at Kasuga Shrine*
  Signature: *Zeshin* and sealed *Koma*

Zeshin made at least two trips to visit the sights
of Nara, the ancient capital south of Kyoto, where
the Kasuga Shrine is located. The lanterns in the
gardens of the shrine and the deer living there
were, and still are, famous.

8 *Herdboy Playing His Flute*
  Signature: *Zeshin* and sealed *Zeshin*

Despite the viscosity of the medium, Zeshin was
able to simulate the fast-moving brushwork of
an ink painting in rendering this classic scene of
a herdboy playing his flute while perched on a
recumbent ox.

47 *Still-Life of Ceramics and Flowers*

Album leaf mounted as a hanging scroll; colored lacquers and gold leaf on prepared paper; 7½ x 6¼ in. (19.1 x 15.9 cm); ca. 1880
Signature: *Zeshin* and sealed *Koma*
Published: Honolulu Academy of Arts (1996), no. 80, p. 176

This painting is a fine example of Zeshin's ability to reproduce different surfaces in lacquer. In the foreground is a Kyoto-ware stoneware ewer; on its side a panel set against a brocade ground depicts a crane beneath a pine tree on the seashore. Behind the ewer trails a cut branch of flowering camellia, and on a stand to the left a large Tamba-ware jar holds branches of plum blossom.

The ewer is reminiscent of wares such as those made by Aoki Mokubei (1767–1833) and Nin'ami Dōhachi (1783–1855), which imitated earlier ceramics from China, Korea, and Japan, and were favored for tea gatherings in the nineteenth century. The surface of the ewer is rendered in a range of colored lacquers, among which rare and expensive white lacquer predominates.

Also popular among tea-ceremony aficionados were the dark brown textured surfaces and lustrous amber-brown glazes of Tamba, Seto, and Bizen ceramics, such as tea-powder containers (*cha-ire*), flower vases, and fresh-water containers. These made ideal models for Zeshin to reproduce in lacquer, and he did so on numerous occasions, not only in painting but also as *cha-ire*-form *sagemono* (see no. 21).

48 *Still-Life of Doll Festival Figures in Preparation*

Hanging scroll, colored lacquers, white pigment, and gold leaf on paper; 12½ x 16½ in. (31.8 x 41.9 cm)
Signature: *Zeshin* and sealed *Koma*

In an unusual take on a popular traditional theme, Zeshin has created a still-life of doll-heads in the process of being prepared for the Doll Festival. Nine clay heads, in various stages of finish, are ranged on the presumed working surface on the right, the artist's tools and materials below them on the left: two brushes, an ink stick, an inkstone, and a ceramic water dropper in the shape of a chrysanthemum blossom. The fact that Zeshin has left some of the heads featureless, as though he was interrupted while painting them, is typical of his sense of humor. Zeshin made a number of studies of this image, and there is a lacquer painting of the same subject mounted in an album.[1]

This painting was once owned by the Tamura family of Ashikaya who sold it at the Tokyo Dealers' Association in 1928.[2]

1. See Gōke (1981a), vol. 1, no. 28.
2. Sasaki and Sasaki (2003), no. 5415, p. 1305.

49 *Decorated Cowrie Shells*

Hanging scroll, colored lacquers and applied
mother-of-pearl fragments on prepared paper;
12¼ x 14⅛ in. (31.1 x 36.5 cm); ca. 1880
Signature: *Zeshin* and sealed *Tairyūkyo*

According to the inscription on the storage box,
decorated cowrie shells were traditionally given
to pregnant women to serve as a talisman for a
successful birth. While images of shells are frequently encountered in Zeshin's work, they are
usually those found scattered along the shoreline,
not the painted cowries pictured here.

50 *Evergreen Oak Tree over Stream*

Hanging scroll, colored lacquer on paper; 10⅞ x
16¾ in. (27.6 x 42.5 cm)
Signed: *Zeshin* and sealed *Shin*
Published: Gōke (1981a), vol. 1, pl. 156

The gnarled trunk of an ancient evergreen oak
(*kashi*) is shown growing over a meandering
stream. A branch of aging, insect-eaten leaves
hangs down, painted in greens and yellows. A
very hard wood, *kashi* has long been used for
making wood swords, not just as fencing swords
for martial arts, but also for doctors' swords and
similar weapons (see no. 23).

Not only did Zeshin have the ability to paint
in lacquer, he was also able to mix in color pigment, enabling him to create polychrome images
such as this. The blacks, browns, yellows, greens,
and earth tones that resulted were of great appeal
to Zeshin's clientele (see also nos. 49, 51, and 52).

51 *Cricket and Flowering Vine*

Hanging scroll, colored lacquers and gold wash
on prepared paper; 13⅛ x 18 in. (34 x 45.7 cm);
ca. 1880
Signature: *Zeshin* and sealed *Koma*
Published: Shibata (1912), n.p. (4th leaf from the
back); Honolulu Academy of Arts (1996), no. 79,
p. 174

The contrast between the freely drawn vine stem
and the minutely detailed insect in this painting
is an example of Zeshin's ability to switch styles
in order to enhance the effect of an image. The
gold wash background suggests the glow of eve-
ning. Flowering gourds and the sound of crickets
are traditional harbingers of autumn in Japan. The
seasonal mood here is enhanced by the overall
brown and yellow palette and the pooling of the
lacquer on the leaves. The petal weighed down
by the insect is a particularly effective touch.[1]

1. A related preparatory drawing depicting a locust on a
gourd vine is illustrated in Gōke (1981b), no. 3, p. 71.

52 *Bat and* Reishi *Fungus*

Hanging scroll, colored lacquer on paper; 14½ x
20 in. (36.8 x 50.8 cm); 1879
Signature: *Gyōnen nanajūsan-ō* (at the age of sev-
enty-three) *Tairyūkyo Zeshin* and sealed *Moku* (?)

The generalized sentiment expressed here is a
wish for long life and good fortune. In East Asia
fungus (*Polyporus lucidus*) is thought to live for
one thousand years and is thus a symbol of
longevity. Because in Chinese, the character for
fu, or bat, is pronounced in the same way as the
character for "good fortune," bats are considered messengers of good luck.

Zeshin first began to paint in lacquer in 1872,
but it was not until the last decade of his life that
he started to produce large numbers of hanging
scrolls and miniature paintings for inclusion in
small albums. The present work is one of the
earlier examples and with its swirling layers of
different colored lacquers, is a technical tour-de-
force.

The mounting is a trompe l'oeil version of the
standard mounting for a hanging scroll (cf. nos.
35, 37). It was painted on silk by Zeshin's student
Shōji Chikushin, and represents the Attributes of
the Seven Gods of Good Fortune, in keeping
with the theme of the image.

This painting was once the property of the
Ishikawa family of Osaka who sold it at auction
at the Tokyo Dealers' Association in 1932.[1]

1. Sasaki and Sasaki (2004), no. 177, p. 43.

53 *Heron and Crow in Flight*

Hanging scroll, colored lacquers, white pigment, and gold leaf on paper; 16½ x 23⅞ in. (41.9 x 60.6 cm); ca. 1880
Signature: *Zeshin sei* and sealed *Tairyūkyo*; the rollers signed *Tai Shin* [Ikeda Taishin]
Provenance: Fujioka Family collection, sold Tokyo Art Dealers Association, 24 May, 1920

During the Tenpō era (1830–44), Zeshin moved from Tachibana-chō to Kami Heiemon in Asakusa, in the northeast of Edo. Opposite his home, on the south bank of the Kanda River, was an earthen embankment with a row of large, old willow trees growing on it, hence its name Yanagihara (Willow moor). Zeshin is said to have delighted in observing the local vegetation and wild life that characterized the spot, and the name "Residence Facing Willow Trees" (*Tairyūkyo*), which appears here as his seal, commemorates it. Herons wading in the river or perched on the branches of the willows would have been a familiar sight, as would

the spectacle of birds in flight above the river, taking off or coming into land.

Contrasting the heron's white plumage with the black of the crow's is a typical Zeshin conceit, one he used in a number of works, both in lacquerware (for example, a tiered box now in the Tokyo National Museum) and in other paintings.[1]

This hanging scroll was once owned by the Fujioka family, of Nagano Prefecture. They were important patrons of Zeshin and possessed a number of his works, which were sold at auction in Tokyo in 1920.[2]

1. For the lacquer box, see Gōke (1981a), vol. 1, pls. 1, 2; and idem, for two panels once mounted as a floor screen, pls. 142, 143.
2. Sasaki and Sasaki (2003), no. 5035, p. 1215.

APPENDIX

No. 44 *Additional album leaves*

44-6

44-2

44-3

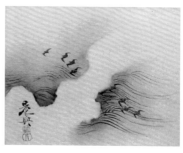
44-4

44-5

44-7

44-8

44-9

44-10

44-11

44-12

44-13

44-14

44-15

44-16

44-17

44-19

44-20

44-21

44-22

44-23

44-24

44-25

44-26

44-27

44-28

44-29

44-31

44-33

44-34

44-35

44-37

44-38

44-39

44-40

44-41

44-42

44-43

44-44

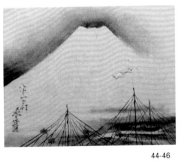

44-45

44-46

45-1

45-2

44-7

45-4

45-6

45-7

45-8

45-10

45-12

45-13

45-15

45-18

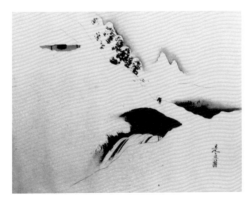

45-19

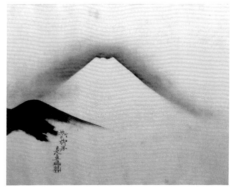

45-20

Signatures and Seals

Lacquerware

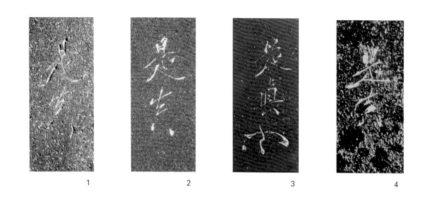

1 2 3 4

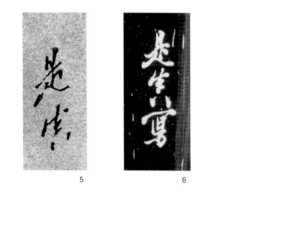

5 6 7 8

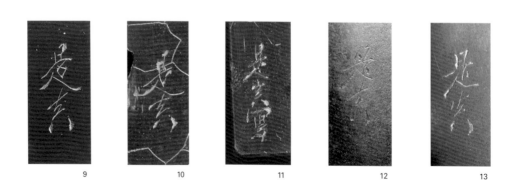

9 10 11 12 13

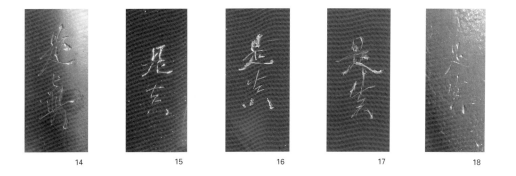

14   15   16   17   18

19   20   21

Scabbard 22   *Fuchi* 22   23

24   Lid 25   Alternate lid 25   26   27

28 29

30 31 33

32

  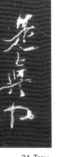

34 Jubako 34 Tray 34 Sake cup

35

36

37

38 left

38 right

39

40

41

42

43

47

48

49

50

51

52

53

GLOSSARY

binan kazura: "Climbing vine of handsome men" (*Kadsura japonica*), a Japanese flowering quince, used in the Edo period (1615–1868) as a pomade, hence its nickname.

bokutō: A wood sword, known as a "doctor's sword."

bon: Tray.

bunjinga: Literati painting.

cha-ire: Tea powder container.

chūban: Medium size print, approximately 10½ x 8 in. (26.7 x 20.3 cm).

chūmawashi: The area of decorative silk which surrounds the image and the *ichimonji* on a traditional Japanese painting mount.

fubako: A type of document box.

fuchi: A ferrule: one of a pair of sword-fittings placed on either end of the handle, the other being the *kashira*, or cap.

fundame: Very fine gold powder densely sprinkled onto a wet lacquer ground. Since it is too fine to be polished, the resulting surface is smooth and matt.

fūtai: The two strips of silk which hang down from the top of a traditional Japanese painting mount.

Gosekku: The five traditional festivals: *Oshōgatsu*, celebrated on New Year's day; *Hina-matsuri*, Doll Festival, celebrated on the third day of the third month; *Tango no sekku*, Boy's Festival, celebrated on the fifth day of the fifth month; *Tanabata*, the star festival; *Choyo no sekku*, the chrysanthemum festival, celebrated on the ninth day of the ninth month.

haikai: A genre of popular linked verse which flourished in the early Edo period.

hako: Box.

hana-ire: A flower vase.

harigaki: A technique used by Zeshin to engrave small areas of the design and to scratch his signature, for which he employed a rat's tooth mounted on a handle.

heidai: Cupstand.

heishi: Ewer.

Hina-matsuri: Doll Festival, held on the third day of the third month.

himotoshi: The cord channels of an *inrō*.

hiramaki-e: Literally "flat sprinkled picture," metal or colored powders sprinkled onto a lacquer ground before it has hardened, usually covered with a protective layer of transparent lacquer.

hokku: Seventeen-syllable poetry also known as haiku.

ichimonji: The narrow strips of decorated silk at the top and bottom of the image on a traditional Japanese painting mount.

iki: An aesthetic and moral concept held in high regard by Zeshin and his audience (see Introduction).

inrō: A tiered, decorative carrying container worn suspended from a sash from the late sixteenth century onwards.

kadō: A traditional art of flower appreciation that has flourished in Japan since the sixteenth century, also known as ikebana.

kakihan: A paraph or cursive monogram, often used in place of a signature or seal by Japanese artists.

kanshitsu: Dry lacquer technique whereby fabric or similar material is soaked with lacquer, applied to a prepared mold and removed once hardened.

kashi: Evergreen oak (*Quercus myrsinæfolia*), a hardwood found in Japan and China.

kashibako: A box for cakes.

kashira: Cap: one of a pair of sword-fittings placed on either end of the handle, the other being the *fuchi*, or ferrule.

katabami: Wood sorrel (*Oxalis acetosella*), a plant well-known in Japan for its medicinal properties and use as a polish for bronze mirrors.

katakiri-bori: A technique used in lacquer and metal to simulate brush painting. The carved groove has a V-shaped cross-section with one side longer and shallower than the other.

kōdō: A traditional art of incense appreciation that has flourished in Japan since the fifteenth century.

kōgō: Small incense container.

koiguchi: Literally "carp mouth": the fitting at the opening of a sword scabbard.

kojiri: The cap for the bottom of a sword scabbard.

kome: Cooked rice.

koshirae: The complete set of decorative mounts for a sword.

kozuka: The auxiliary knife and its handle which is fitted into the outside wall of a sword scabbard.

kurikata: The cord ring on a sword scabbard.

kyōka: Comic, or "crazy," verse.

jūbako: A tiered box to hold food.

machibori: A city metalworker who manufactured fittings for sale to the public, rather than on a commission basis; his work was usually signed.

maki-e: "Sprinkled picture," a generic term for a number of related lacquer techniques in which metal or colored powders are sprinkled onto wet lacquer.

manju: A Japanese rice cake.

menuki: Decorative metal ornaments each side of a sword hilt to enhance the grip.

meshi: Uncooked rice.

mitate-e: Parodic images which included incongruous elements but which recall famous literary or historic scenes through a contemporary lens.

mizusashi: Pure water container used in the rituals associated with the drinking of powdered green tea.

nashiji: A lacquer surface resembling pear skin.

Niō-mon: The traditional temple gate guarded by a pair of Deva-kings.

ojime: Bead, used as a slide to tighten the cords on an *inrō*.

omodaka: Water plantain (*Sagittaria trifolia*), a tri-lobe-leafed plant which grows in rice-paddies and other wet, marshy areas.

rōgin: Lacquer simulating an alloy of silver and copper with a high silver content, polished to a gloss finish.

ryōshibako: Stationery box.

sadō: The ritualized preparation and serving of powdered green tea.

sagemono: A collective term for pouches and containers worn suspended from a sash.

sakazuki: Wine cup.

seidō-nuri: Lacquer surface simulating bronze thought to have been invented by Zeshin during the 1840s.

seigaiha-nuri: A combed lacquer surface resembling the waves of the sea, said to have been originated by Seigai Kanshichi in the late 17th century, and revived by Zeshin during the 1840s.

seppa: Thin brass, copper, gold, or lacquer washers placed on either side of a sword guard when mounted on a sword.

sha: Copied.

shakudo: A metal alloy of approximately 95% copper and 5% gold with a blue-black appearance often used for sword-fittings.

shasei: Realistic observation.

shibuichi: A metal alloy of copper and silver with a silvery-grey appearance often used for sword-fittings.

shikishiban: Rectangular paper format for inscribing poetry.

shishiaimaki-e: A combination of *maki-e* techniques, most notably *hiramaki-e* and *takamaki-e*.

shitan: Chinese rosewood.

shitan-nuri: Lacquer surface simulating Chinese rosewood thought to have been invented by Zeshin in the 1840s.

shūmon-nuri: Lacquer surface simulating the surface of roughly hewn stoneware ceramics that Zeshin revived in the 1840s.

surimono: "Printed thing," a privately commissioned print that was distributed to commemorate special events or the New Year.

suzuribako: A box for brushes, ink, ink-stone, water-dropper, and other writing implements.

takamaki-e: "High sprinkled picture," similar to *hiramaki-e*, but parts of the design are raised by the addition of clay or charcoal powder.

takaramono: The myriad treasures associated with the Seven Gods of Good Fortune.

tantō: Short sword.

tenchi: The two panels of decorative silk, usually matching, at the top and bottom of a traditional Japanese painting mount.

tetsusabi-nuri: Lacquer surface simulating rusty iron that Zeshin invented during the 1840s.

tonkotsu: Tobacco container worn suspended from the sash.

ukiyo-e: "Pictures of the floating world." School of genre painting featuring images of actors, courtesans, and others, which emerged in the late 17th century.

urushi: Lacquer.

urushi-e: Lacquer picture, usually on paper, applied directly with a brush rather than sprinkled on as in *maki-e*.

utsutsu: Copied.

Yamato-e: Japanese painting in traditional style.

yamimaki-e: Literally "dark sprinkled picture," *maki-e* whereby black or brown powders are sprinkled onto a dark lacquer ground.

BIBLIOGRAPHY

Bushell, Raymond. 1979. *The Inrō Handbook: Studies of Netsuke, Inrō, and Lacquer.* New York and Tokyo: Weatherhill.

Dilworth, David and J. Thomas Rimer, eds. 1977. *The Historical Fiction of Mori Ōgai.* (Honolulu: University of Hawaii Press).

Dresser, Christopher. 1882. *Japan: Its Architecture, Art, and Art Manufacture.* London: Longmans, Green and Co. Reprint as *Traditional Arts and Crafts of Japan.* New York: Dover Publications, 1994.

Dunn, Michael. 2001. *Five Tastes: Traditional Japanese Design.* Exh. cat. New York: Japan Society, Harry N. Abrams.

Earle, Joe. 1996. "Shibata Zeshin: Technique, Style, and Dating," in Earle, ed. (1996), pp. 24–35.

Earle, Joe, ed. 1986. *The Toshiba Gallery: Japanese Art and Design.* London: Victoria and Albert Museum.

———. 1996. *Meiji no Takara: Treasures of Imperial Japan. Masterpieces by Shibata Zeshin (The Nasser D. Khalili Collection of Japanese Art).* London: Kibo Foundation.

———. 1997. *Shibata Zeshin: Masterpieces of Japanese Lacquer from the Khalili Collection.* Exh. cat. London: Kibo Foundation.

Eskenazi. 1996. *Japanese Inrō and Lacquer-ware from a Private Swedish Collection.* Exh. cat. London: Eskenazi.

Foulds, Martin. 1977. "Zeshin's Life and Works." In Honolulu Academy of Arts (1977), pp. 19–30.

Fujioka Sakutarō. 1910. *Kinsei kaigashi* (A history of painting in recent times). Tokyo: Kinkōdō Shōseki.

Gōke Tadaomi. 1981a. *Bakumatsu kaikaki no shikkō kaiga: Shibata Zeshin meihinshū* (Lacquer and paintings in the late Edo and early Meiji: A collection of masterworks by Shibata Zeshin). Tokyo: Gakken.

———. 1981b. *Shibata Zeshin eyo tebikae* (Sketches and notes by Shibata Zeshin). Tokyo: Dōbōsha.

Hart, Ernest. 1887. *Lectures on Japanese Art Work, 1886.* London: Society for the Encouragement of Arts, Manufactures, and Commerce.

Helmut-Corvey, Theodor, ed. 1997. *Inrō: Das Ding am Gürtel. Japanische Medizindöschen aus der Sammlung Heinz und Else Kress.* Exh. cat. Bielefeld: Kerber Verlag.

Honolulu Academy of Arts. 1979. *The Art of Shibata Zeshin: The Mr. and Mrs. James E O'Brien Collection at the Honolulu Academy of Arts.* Essays by Mary Louise O'Brien and Martin Foulds. Catalogue by Howard A. Link. [London]: Robert G. Sawers Publishing in association with the Honolulu Academy of Arts.

Honolulu Academy of Arts. 1996. *Shadows and Reflections: Japanese Lacquer from the Collection of Edmund J. Lewis at the Honolulu Academy of Arts.* Exh. cat. [Honolulu]: Honolulu Academy of Arts.

Hutt, Julia. 1997. *Japanese Inrō.* Victoria and Albert Museum: Far Eastern Series. New York: Weatherhill.

Kawasaki Chitora. 1897. "Zeshin." *Kokka* 97 (Oct. 1897), pp. 3–7.

Kuki Shūzō, 1930. *"Iki" no kōzō* (The structure of "*iki*"). Tokyo: Iwanami Shoten. Eng. Ed.: Kuki Shūzō. *Reflections on Japanese Taste: The Structure of Iki.* Trans. John Clark. Ed. Sakuto Matsui and John Clark. Sydney: Power Publications. 1997.

Lazarnick, George. 1982. *Netsuke and Inrō Artists and How to Read their Signatures.* Honolulu: Reed Publishers.

Link, Howard A. 1979. Catalogue, in Honolulu Academy of Arts (1979), pp. 31–177.

Meech, Julia. 1995. *Lacquerware from the Weston Collection.* New York: Christie's.

Narazaki Muneshige, ed. 1988. *British Museum III.* Vol. 3 *Ukiyo-e Masterpieces in European Collections.* Tokyo: Kodansha.

Sasaki Jōhei and Sasaki Masako. 2003. *Photographic Archive of Japanese Paintings: Maruyama Shijō School, 4.* Tokyo: Kogasōran.

———. 2004. *Photographic Archive of Japanese Paintings: Maruyama Shijō School, 5.* Tokyo: Kogasōran.

Schaap, Robert, ed. 1987. *Meiji: Japanese Art in Transition: Ceramics, Cloisonné, Lacquer, Prints, Illustrated Books, Drawings and Paintings from the Meiji period (1868–1912).* Exh. cat. The Hague: Haags Gemeentemuseum.

Shibata Kametarō. 1912. *Zeshin-ō gakan zokuhen* (An illustrated survey of the Venerable Zeshin, continued). Tokyo: Gahōsha.

Shioda Shin, ed. 1908. *Zeshin-ō gakan* (An illustrated survey of the Venerable Zeshin). Tokyo: Gahōsha.

Sotheby Parke Bernet. 1977. *Highly Important Japanese Prints, Illustrated Books, Drawings and Paintings from the Henri Vever Collection: Part III.* London: Sotheby Parke Bernet.

Stern, Harold P. 1972. *The Magnificent Three: Lacquer, Netsuke, and Tsuba. Selections from the Collection of Charles A. Greenfield.* Exh. cat. New York: Japan Society.

Umezawa Ryūshin. 1996. "A Brief Biography of Shibata Zeshin." In Earle, Joe, ed. (1996), pp. 36–63.

Watson, William, ed. 1981. *The Great Japan Exhibition: Art of the Edo Period, 1600–1868.* Exh. cat. London: Royal Academy of Arts, in association with Weidenfeld and Nicolson.

Watt, James C. Y., and Barbara Ford. 1991. *East Asian Lacquer: The Florence and Herbert Irving Collection.* Exh. cat. New York: The Metropolitan Museum of Art.

Yamane Yuzō, et al. 1980. *Bunjinga shoga* (Literati painting and other schools). Vol. 6, *Zaigai Nihon no Shihō* (Treasures of Japan abroad). Tokyo: Mainichi Shimbunsha.

———. 1981. *Kōgei* (Applied arts). Vol. 10, *Zaigai Nihon no shihō* (Treasures of Japan abroad). Tokyo: Mainichi Shimbunsha.

Yokomizo Hiroko and Satsuma Masato. 2005. *Shibata Zeshin shita-e shaseishō / Sketches by Shibata Zeshin—within the Collection of the University Art Museum, Tokyo National University of Fine Arts and Music.* Osaka: Tōhō Shuppansha.

Yonemura, Ann. 1979. *Japanese Lacquer.* Exh. cat. Washington, D.C.: Freer Gallery of Art, Smithsonian Institution.

Yonemura, Ann. 1997. Introduction to *Twelve Centuries of Japanese Art from the Imperial Collections.* Exh. cat. Washington, D.C.: Freer Gallery of Art and the Arthur M. Sackler Gallery, Smithsonian Institution.

ACKNOWLEDGMENTS

My thanks go first to Kay and Tom Edson for giving me the opportunity to write the catalogue of their Zeshin collection, sharing as I do their own enthusiasm for the artist's work. I am also grateful to Marion Oettinger, Jr., Director of the San Antonio Museum of Art, and Martha Blackwelder, Maddux-Cowden-Brown Curator of Asian Art at the museum, for their support of both the exhibition and this publication.

Over the years I have been indebted to a number of colleagues for encouraging my interest in Zeshin and providing practical assistance: in Tokyo, Masaharu Nagano, Mitsuru Tajima, and Toshiyuki Hara; and in London, Patrick Syz.

Joe Earle, Matsutaro Shoriki Chair of the Department of Art of Asia, Oceania, and Africa at the Museum of Fine Arts, Boston, who has contributed the Introduction to the catalogue, has generously shared his knowledge of lacquer and of Zeshin's work in particular. John T. Carpenter, Lecturer in the History of Japanese Art, School of Oriental and African Studies, University of London, has supplied the translations in numbers 6 and 23, and elucidated the split inscription in the former, a conceit in keeping with its function as a writing box.

For permission to reproduce their painting by Maruyama Ōkyo in figure 2, my thanks go to Constance Miller and the J. Sanford and Constance Miller Foundation, as they do to Emily Sano, Director, Asian Art Museum of San Francisco, and her staff for supplying the photo. The woodblock print of a lacquer workshop in figure 1 is reproduced by permission of the Victoria and Albert Museum, London, and I am grateful to Julia Hutt for facilitating this. Acknowledgments are also due to Andrew Keelan of the Nourhouse Foundation for granting permission to quote in the Introduction translations of the two *haikai* by Zeshin, originally published in *Meiji no Takara: Treasures of Imperial Japan. Masterpieces by Shibata Zeshin (The Nasser D. Khalili Collection of Japanese Art)*.

Writing the catalogue has inevitably taken its toll on other projects, and I thank my colleagues in New York, Kathryn Williamson and Geoffrey R. Dunn, for their patience and cooperation during this time. In the task of realizing the catalogue, I am deeply indebted to the editorial assistance of Mary Laing, and to the skill and dedication of the designer, Miki Aoyagi. I am also grateful to Julia Meech and Jane Oliver for taking the time to read the text and commenting upon it. Finally, I would also like to express my appreciation to the photographers, Peggy Tenison, John Deane, and Douglas Chew Ho, for their excellent work, and to Brandy Young, the typesetter, and Desiree Bucks and her team at Pressroom, Hong Kong, for their professionalism and commitment to the project.

Sebastian Izzard